The Prediction Book of Divination

The Prediction Book of

DIVINATION

Jo Logan and Lindsay Hodson

BLANDFORD PRESS
POOLE · DORSET

First published in the U.K. 1984 by Blandford Press,
Link House, West Street, Poole, Dorset, BH15 1LL.

Distributed in the United States by
Sterling Publishing Co., Inc.,
2 Park Avenue, New York, N.Y. 10016.

British Library Cataloguing in Publication Data

Hodson, Lindsay
  The prediction book of divination.
  1. Fortune-Telling
  I. Title   II. Logan, Jo
  133.3'24'028   BF1861

ISBN 0 7137 1398 4

Typeset by Poole Typesetting (Wessex) Ltd.
Printed in Great Britain by Butler & Tanner Ltd., Frome and London

Contents

Introduction

Divination, in one form or another, has been practised from the earliest times on record and is still prevalent today in every country of the world. The method used may vary considerably according to numerous factors, such as the materials available, the temperament of the diviner, the object of the exercise, the traditions of the culture in which it is being practised and so on. Yet the ultimate aim of any form of divination is always the same: discovery of the future or otherwise unknown events by supernatural means.

Divination can, of course, be carried out at various levels, too. To some people it may appear to be little more than a game, a bit of harmless fun that might, just might, provide an indication of something that has yet to happen. At the other end of the scale, divination may be regarded as a way of communing with supernatural forces, forging links with arcane knowledge outside man's normal comprehension but which, with practice, can become accessible if not explainable in scientific terms.

Man is a curious animal and the techniques he has devised to help him gain insight into the unknown have assumed a great variety of forms over the centuries. Yet, whatever technique is employed, no matter what approach the diviner takes to the whole subject, divination is a method of gaining access to the supernormal; it is, by definition, a means of acquiring insight.

Each of us has psychic abilities even if we are not consciously aware of the fact: we are all, to a lesser or greater degree, sensitive to non-physical forces. We are all capable, therefore, of developing such abilities and one way of doing so is through divination.

Cartomancy

What we now refer to as ordinary playing cards derive from the Tarot, the origins of which are shrouded in mystery and confusion. So much so, in fact, that we can only surmise at its source because, despite the numerous theories that abound, the Tarot's history cannot be traced back any earlier than the 14th century with accuracy.

Be that as it may, the fact remains that cards – in one form or another – have been used for divinatory purposes for centuries. Tarot cards, in particular, are associated with divination and have long been considered as much more than mere pieces of pasteboard used for playing parlour games. Although the Tarot is regarded with a certain amount of awe by some people, playing cards – which are a familiar part of most people's lives – are not so readily identified as sources of arcane wisdom. Yet playing cards, too, are intrinsically symbolic.

Indeed, in some ways it is easier to recognise the basic correspondences implicit in a deck of playing cards than it is in a Tarot pack consisting of 78 cards divided into Major and Minor Arcana. For instance, the fact that the modern deck comprises 52 cards immediately puts one in mind of the number of weeks in a year; the four suits can be ascribed to the four seasons or the four elements; the 13 cards in each suit correspond to the number of lunar months in a year as well as the weeks in each quarter; there are 12 court cards, just as there are 12 calendar months and 12 signs of the zodiac; and so on.

Thus it can be seen that a pack of modern playing cards contains as much symbolism as does the Tarot from which it derives, it is simply not thought of primarily in this way by those who regard it as a game-playing medium. Yet, to others, such a familiar object has hidden meanings which carry as much weight as any other divinatory tool and its use as such will help to heighten your sensitivity: your powers of observation, intuition and prophetic abilities.

The meanings of the cards

The four suits, like those of the Tarot, are associated with different aspects of life:

Clubs – practical pursuits, business affairs.
Diamonds – financial matters, prestige and influence.
Hearts – emotional considerations such as love, romance and affection.
Spades – problems, obstacles and challenges.

Each suit consists of 13 cards, three court cards and ten numbered or pip cards. In general terms, the court cards represent people or their thoughts whereas the pip cards refer to actual events, situations, changing circumstances and possibilities. Every card has a specific meaning in a spread and this relates to its numerical/face value as well as to the suit to which it belongs.

It is important to remember, though, that it is not sufficent simply to learn the exact meanings of each card, every spread must be interpreted in the light of certain other considerations if any degree of accuracy is to be obtained. These include the positions in which the cards fall, the matter under consideration and, most importantly, the personal circumstances and, if possible, characteristics of the person for whom the reading is being carried out.

This latter point is why some interpreters choose to use a significator – a card to represent the enquirer or querent – as this helps to focus the consultant's faculties on the individual concerned when considering the various aspects of the spread. The significator is chosen from the 12 court cards to approximate as closely as possible to the age, sex and physical or temperamental characteristics of the querent.

Age and sex
  King – a mature man.
  Queen – a mature woman.
  Jack – a young person of either sex.

Physical characteristics
  Clubs – people with rich brown or red hair, a high colour and brown or hazel eyes. An active, energetic personality.
  Diamonds – very fair people with pale skins, fair or white hair and light blue or grey eyes. Assured, sophisticated people.
  Hearts – light brown or auburn haired people with fair, pinkish complexions and blue, grey or hazel eyes. A friendly, sympathetic nature.

Spades – sallow complexioned people with dark brown or black hair and dark eyes. A powerful or influential person, a strong character.

Sometimes, of course, the physical appearance of the enquirer is unknown – a postal reading, for instance – and the significator's suit will then be chosen according to the nature of the enquiry *(see* page 10).

Even if the sex of the querent is unknown the Ace of the selected suit can be used to represent him/her because this card is believed to embody the very essence of the suit itself.

Another point worth considering is that no card of itself can be good or bad, it merely carries the potentiality for positive and negative responses. For example, if the Eight of Spades, signifying obstacles, turns up in a prominent position in a spread for someone contemplating going into business for himself, this can be viewed in two ways. The querent may, for instance, decide to abandon his plans as hopeless or regard the obstacle as a challenge to be overcome and use his ingenuity to find a way round it.

This emphasises a very important point which should never be overlooked. The interpreter has a responsibility to present information in a way that will not cause unnecessary distress, worry or fear. This does not mean that warning signals should be ignored or glossed over, far from it, but they should be presented in a constructive manner and, more importantly, in the correct context, not blown up out of all proportion.

There are always other factors to take into consideration – alternatives, helpful influences, how important this particular aspect is to the enquirer, what resources are available and so on. Each spread must be read as a whole, in the light of all available information.

Obviously, when first starting to read the cards, knowing their basic meanings will have to suffice. Yet you will find that the very act of using them for divinatory purposes heightens your powers of intuition – everyone has these faculties although they are not always consciously encouraged – so that, with practice, it becomes easier to interpret spreads and to make the necessary connections between one card and another.

It is therefore a good idea to practise shuffling and laying out the cards in order to familiarise yourself with them before attempting to read them for others. Also, the more frequently a pack of cards is used for this purpose the more quickly it will be imbued with the correct vibrations; this is why they should be kept solely for this purpose. Never use the divinatory deck for card games, it should be handled only by yourself and those for whom you do readings otherwise the energies so carefully built up will be dissipated.

Having said all that, here are the individual meanings of the cards.

Clubs

King A man who is neither fair nor dark. A kind and helpful friend or adviser, most likely a relative of a female enquirer and a work colleague or associate of a male querent. Probably a professional man of some standing, he is faithful and loyal to his friends and shows integrity in his business dealings.

Queen A warm-hearted woman of middle years, possibly a widow, a close friend of a woman enquirer. If the querent is a male, this card signifies his wife or a close confidante. In either case, this person is well-intentioned towards the querent and can offer practical advice as well as comfort.

Jack A reliable friend of either sex who admires the questioner and wishes to help him/her. If the querent is a female, this card could indicate that she is very much in this person's thoughts. For either sex, it also means that any petty annoyances that may arise should be ignored as they will soon disappear.

Ten A very auspicious card signifying happiness and good fortune, it can counterbalance bad influences shown in other cards. Indicative of unexpected money coming your way, perhaps a legacy or winnings, it may refer to a long journey which, whether for business or pleasure, will prove surprisingly successful.

Nine A very ambivalent card: it may indicate financial gain, an unexpected opportunity or marriage; or it can signify business problems, disagreements and obstinacy resulting in loss of prestige. It should, therefore, be regarded as a possible warning against ignoring the wishes of others.

Eight A social invitation which you feel unsure about accepting – go ahead, it will bring pleasure and may lead to a new romantic attachment. Alternatively, a new business venture which you will undertake with friends or present associates; this promises well as long as no financial gambles are taken.

Seven If surrounding cards are good, it promises prosperity and success but there must be no interference or opposition from the opposite sex. The signing of an important document or contract; take legal advice if you have any doubts. There could be minor worries or delays but these can be overcome.

Six   A success card pertaining to business, usually associated with a partnership. A new friend will come into your circle who could prove helpful in business matters, either financially or in an advisory capacity. A good time to lay the foundations for your children's future prosperity and security.

Five   Parties and social gatherings could lead to a new friendship that will bring benefits. A marriage or liaison with a wealthy mate, resulting in greater prosperity for both partners. News from abroad could cause initial concern but this will be due mainly to misunderstanding the situation.

Four   A friend may let you down unexpectedly, so be prepared for disappointment. There is also danger of loss due to unforeseen circumstances or the treachery or deceit of others, so make sure you have contingency plans ready and guard against false promises. Check other cards for offsetting influences.

Three   If a querent has been married previously, this card signifies remarriage or at least a proposal. It also promises marriage or a romantic liaison for someone whose prolonged close emotional links with another have been broken. In either case, the new partnership should prove happy and successful.

Two   A time of change and uncertainty when it would be unwise to make any rash moves. Keep a wary eye on your budget as there could be unexpected bills to be met. Relationships, too, could be under a bit of a strain, so try to restrain your tongue or you may find that you say things that you will regret later.

Ace   A financial gain of some sort, perhaps as a result of a legacy, winning gamble or unexpected gift. This card may also refer to renown or recognition, especially if the querent's occupation puts him/her in the public eye. Whatever the case, the enquirer can expect a letter or papers concerning money to arrive shortly.

Diamonds

King   A strong man of affairs who can be ruthless in business and a dangerous rival in love. For a woman, this card may signify an unfaithful lover or husband; for a male, such a man will put a business proposition to you. For either sex, it warns that over-ambition will be thwarted by another's actions.

Queen   A self-assured woman, fond of society and admiration, who may pose a threat to the querent. For a woman, this card could indicate a jealous rival and, for a man, interference in his business affairs. The message is to make the best use of your abilities and to try to avoid a confrontation.

Jack   A pleasant young man or fair-haired relative who will be the bearer of news. For a female querent, this information may prove unwelcome or upsetting but not disastrous. For both sexes, this card warns against imprudence and dishonesty, perhaps on someone else's part, which could result in loss.

Ten   An unexpected journey or meeting could lead to romance and, eventually, marriage. Finances will be highlighted and, as long as you remain in control of the situation, the end result should see you better off than before. Good common sense and caution now will pay dividends in the future.

Nine   New opportunities will occur. These may refer to a business venture that the querent is considering, a change of job or residence, romance or travel. In any event, the outlook is encouraging and the enquirer should find the wherewithal needed to start new projects or put long-made plans into effect.

Eight   A trip or holiday taken now could have romantic conclusions; alternatively, the querent could marry someone from abroad. Both options apply particularly to very young or elderly enquirers. It is a good time, too, for a little flutter as there are indications of unexpected money luck, though on a small scale.

Seven   This card warns of adverse criticism and gossip. Extreme caution is advised, especially if the querent is thinking of taking a gamble or starting a new project. On the lighter side, it can presage a party or social invitation – pleasant but unimportant pastimes. There could also be some surprising news.

Six   Often, this refers to an early marriage which comes to an end and the chance of a second partnership. It may also denote a reconciliation if there has been an emotional upheaval in the querent's life recently. An unexpected gift from the loved one could help to heal the breach.

14

Five   A card of good omen signifying a successful business undertaking, enduring friendships and great domestic happiness. New ventures are particularly favoured, so it is a good time to lay the foundations for future security. There is also a possibility that the querent will receive news of a birth shortly.

Four   Important changes are imminent. In general, things should improve, especially if the querent has been suffering some stress and strain lately due to frustrations and disagreements. Family and friends should be more co-operative in the future and the whole outlook is very encouraging.

Three Not a very helpful card. Partnerships are likely to be under a strain. If married, this could refer to marital disputes or domestic problems. Business associates, too, may not be very co-operative. There is a strong possibility of legal action although this does not necessarily imply an adverse outcome.

Two   A new love affair could meet with disapproval or opposition from family or friends, thus causing friction, so great tact will be needed. Changes generally are in the air, so expect new developments in business life, too. These can be used to advantage as long as you are prepared to work hard.

Ace   Exciting news is on its way, perhaps indicating a proposal of marriage for a female querent, the successful conclusion of a business deal for a male or, for the younger generation, the passing of an examination. Alternatively, this card may presage an unexpected gift or small inheritance.

Hearts

King   A fair, aristocratic man or an influential man who wishes to help the querent. He is affectionate and generous but may be inclined to make rash judgements as he does tend to possess more zeal than discretion. If adversely placed, this card may refer to minor financial problems but these will be short-lived.

Queen A fair woman, loving and lovable, who is kindly disposed towards the querent. If the enquirer is a man, this card refers to his true love or amour; for a woman, a trustworthy friend of the same sex. If adversely placed, however, it warns the querent to beware of rivalry, especially for a woman.

Jack   A fair-haired young person of either sex whose intentions must be divined from the cards on either side of this one. Either a close personal friend of many years' standing or, if newly met, a lover. A chance encounter could lead to a new romance; alternatively, important news is on its way.

Ten   A sign of good fortune, happiness and success combined with an element of surprise. This ten counterbalances any adverse cards in its vicinity and confirms good ones. It also bodes well for romantic prospects and family affairs, especially anything concerning children.

Nine   Traditionally known as the wish card, it promises success in whatever venture is uppermost in the querent's mind at the time of the reading. Even if accompanied by inauspicious cards, it signifies that obstacles can be overcome. Any quarrels or misunderstandings will be resolved and the romantic outlook is rosy.

Eight   An invitation to a social gathering or outing can be expected. Someone met at such an event will prove to be a lifelong friend – even a marriage partner. Romance, pleasures and parties are all on the cards, so are unexpected visitors – a time of enjoyment although one outing may not go exactly as planned.

Seven   Contentment in home life but care will be needed if it is to remain this way. A warning that present plans could go awry due to the unreliability of someone else, so do not rely too heavily on friends or associates at this time. Try to keep plans flexible and be prepared for disappointment.

Six   Good news regarding a child, probably concerning a recent achievement. Unexpected good fortune; romance and a possible proposal or news of a wedding in the family or of a friend. A warning not to let others take advantage of your generosity and good nature or you will be sadly out of pocket.

Five   Family squabbles or problems at work could lead to irritation and a desire for new surroundings but rash moves should be avoided. Try to get a break and think things over calmly before reaching a decision you may otherwise regret. Help or advice could come from an unexpected quarter.

Four   If the querent is an older person, this card could indicate marriage or remarriage. For a younger person, it signifies a change of occupation or residence. In either case, a distinct change of lifestyle is indicated, probably due to a move to a different location, possibly even abroad.

Three   A lack of prudence and tact could lead to difficulties, so it is a time for caution. Try to put off making important decisions until matters improve. If there is a chance of a holiday, take it, even if this means the journey is unplanned, as you will be able to think more clearly after a rest.

Two   This card promises prosperity and success, perhaps greater than anticipated. Even if surrounded by inauspicious cards, this merely indicates a slight delay due to minor obstacles. A new friendship will give much pleasure and could develop into a loving relationship that will lead to marriage.

Ace   This emphasises the home and domestic happiness, but in what way will depend largely on adjacent cards. It may refer to love, friendship, affection and the restoration of domestic harmony or to family squabbles, disruptions and misunderstandings. In any case, news of distant friends or relatives can be expected.

Spades

King   A mature man of position and prestige, probably in one of the professions, especially the law. Very ambitious and unforgiving if crossed, he nevertheless makes a trustworthy and reliable husband or lover. Clear-sighted and logical, he is a superb adviser but tends to have few friends.

Queen   A woman of strong character: independent, self-assured and practical. She may, however, be difficult to get along with as she tends to be too forthright. As a career woman, she is very efficient and may achieve a managerial position but is unlikely to be popular due to lack of genuine warmth.

Jack   A well-meaning acquaintance or relative of either sex with a kindly disposition but inclined to laziness. No matter what this person's age, he/she is emotionally immature and is therefore not to be relied upon, even if pleasant company. A total lack of thoughtfulness could cause friction.

Ten   Not a good omen. This card signifies worries and difficulties, perhaps even grief over the loss of a loved one due to jealousy or lack of understanding. Emotional upheavals will not help the situation, though, and could make matters worse than need be. However, this difficult phase will soon end.

Nine   Disappointing news could cause depression, particularly if the querent is already feeling in low spirits generally. So it is important to take a positive attitude, face facts and start planning for when this difficult period is over. In the meantime, try to conserve your energies and avoid over-exertion.

Eight   This card can presage approaching illness; take normal health precautions and avoid any reckless activities. Business deals or holiday plans are likely to be beset with obstacles or delays, so be prepared for disappointments. An emotional tie, too, could be broken – definitely not a time to force issues.

Seven   Minor difficulties and delays could cause irritation and unnecessary anxiety. There is a real danger that the querent will allow matters to get out of hand, imagining all sorts of disasters and thus encouraging them. It is a time to take stock and decide what is really important and what is not.

Six   Do not be discouraged by present circumstances even if matters seem not to be going according to plan because, despite setbacks, perseverance will pay off in the long run. It may take some time but the promised improvement justifies the effort needed to redress the balance and put things back on an even keel.

Five   A testing time as far as business or money is concerned although you will win through in the end. Emotionally, though, the prospect is more encouraging because this card signifies a happy and successful relationship, so seek support from your loved one who can help you through this awkward patch.

Four   Business worries are likely to be to the fore, so you should get expert advice, particularly if the problem could lead to legal action, because your difficulties will then be resolved more quickly. It's no good relying on friends or partners, though, as emotional relationships may also be tense now.

Three   Partnerships of all kinds are under threat of disruption when this card appears; other cards may indicate which area of the querent's life is most likely to be affected. But, whether business, friendship, romance or marriage, the alliance will suffer from the interference or invervention of a third party.

Two   This card signals the end of one phase and the start of a new. It can indicate a change of residence, job or separation from a loved one (again, adjacent cards may pinpoint the most probable area). Although some form of loss can be expected, the new cycle will bring improvements all round.

Ace   There is a warning that underlying tensions are about to come to the surface. This eruption may be triggered off by thoughtless actions or words yet, in the long term, bringing conflict out into the open will force the querent to face up to challenges and clear the way for making a fresh start.

Special considerations

There are certain combinations of cards that have special meanings if they appear next to one another in a spread. Basically, these can be divided into two main categories and should be interpreted first as they may influence the rest of the reading.

Four, three and two of a kind

Four Aces	Sudden changes, for better or worse depending on other cards.
Four Kings	Promotion and a general improvement in circumstances.
Four Queens	Emphasis falls on social life; pleasures and enjoyment.
Four Jacks	Excitement which should not be allowed to get out of hand.
Four Tens	The attainment of desired aims, especially current wishes.
Four Nines	An unexpected turn of events brings benefits to the querent.
Four Eights	A time of some confusion due to sudden changes of plan.
Four Sevens	Beware of a mischief-maker who may try to cause upsets.
Four Sixes	Unforeseen circumstances could cause hindrance or delay.
Four Fives	Emotional contentment leading to greater future stability.
Four Fours	A changeful situation causes sudden fluctuations of fortune.
Four Threes	An unsettled atmosphere leads to feelings of uncertainty and instability.
Four Twos	The end of one cycle and the start of a better one.
Three Aces	Good news concerning problems of a minor nature.
Three Kings	A co-operative business venture that proves successful.

Three Queens	Entertaining, visits and social occasions involving women.
Three Jacks	Petty annoyances and irritations concerning family or friends.
Three Tens	Financial problems and possible legal action.
Three Nines	Happiness and good fortune; also financial security.
Three Eights	Love, romance and family relationships are highlighted.
Three Sevens	Unwelcome news brings sorrow or disappointment.
Three Sixes	Improved circumstances bring greater stability.
Three Fives	Emotional contentment and personal satisfaction.
Three Fours	Unforeseen opportunities to change one's life-style.
Three Threes	Hopes could be dashed by a third party or outside agency.
Three Twos	Important decisions will have to be made soon.
Two Aces	If Diamonds and Spades, quarrels; otherwise harmonious meetings.
Two Kings	Negotiations or the formation of a business partnership.
Two Queens	A chance meeting; an exchange of ideas or the sharing of a secret.
Two Jacks	Discussions taking place may not be completely above-board.
Two Tens	A change of luck or job, usually for the better.
Two Nines	A substantial gain or improvement of position.
Two Eights	An unlooked for development brings rapid changes.
Two Sevens	Deep, enduring love; also unexpected news.
Two Sixes	Contradictory forces are at work, causing indecision and uncertainty.
Two Fives	Misunderstandings and disagreements confuse the issue.
Two Fours	Circumstances are beyond the querent's direct control.
Two Threes	A choice of direction will cause some serious heart-searching.
Two Twos	A complete break with the past and a fresh start.

Adjacent cards (any order)
Ace of Clubs with a Diamond each side – money coming in.
Ace of Clubs/Nine of Diamonds – legal matters.
Ace of Diamonds with a Diamond each side – financial prosperity.
Ace of Diamonds/Seven of Diamonds/Jack of Diamonds – surprising news.
Ace of Diamonds/Ten of Hearts – a marriage.
Ace of Diamonds/Nine of Spades – a health problem.
Ace of Diamonds/Eight of Clubs – unexpected money.
Ace of Diamonds/Seven of Diamonds – disputes.

Ace of Hearts/Nine of Hearts – emotional happiness.
Ace of Spades/Queen of Clubs – a tiresome journey.
Ace of Spades/Four of Hearts – major change.
Ace of Spades/Nine of Spades – sadness and disappointment.
Ace of Spades/Eight of Spades – problems settled.

King of Clubs/Ten of Clubs – a marriage proposal.
King of Diamonds/Eight of Spades – unexpected journey.
King of Hearts/Nine of Hearts – a love affair.
King of Spades/Seven of Clubs – danger of money loss.

Queen of Clubs/Seven of Diamonds – uncertainty.
Queen of Diamonds/Seven of Diamonds – a serious quarrel.
Queen of Diamonds/Seven of Hearts – jealousy.
Queen of Diamonds/Seven of Spades – a small success.
Queen of Hearts/Ten of Spades – an exciting venture.
Queen of Hearts/Seven of Diamonds – unexpected good news.
Queen of Spades/Jack of Diamonds – a dubious alliance.
Queen of Spades/Jack of Spades – a jealous woman.

Jack of Clubs/Jack of Spades – business difficulties.
Jack of Diamonds/Nine of Spades – bad advice.
Jack of Hearts/Seven of Clubs – a selfish lover.

Ten of Clubs next to any Ace – a large sum of money.
Ten of Clubs next to any Eight – a marriage proposal.
Ten of Diamonds/Eight of Clubs – a romantic journey.
Ten of Diamonds/Seven of Spades – certain delay.
Ten of Hearts next to any King and Queen – news of a wedding.
Ten of Hearts/Nine of Clubs – entertainment.
Ten of Hearts/Ten of Diamonds – a marriage.
Ten of Spades/Seven of Clubs – disappointment of plans.
Ten of Spades next to any Club – major business problems.

Nine of Clubs/Nine of Hearts – a possible legacy.
Nine of Clubs/Eight of Hearts – celebration.
Nine of Diamonds/Ace of Diamonds/Ten of Diamonds – important
news from afar.
Nine of Diamonds/Eight of Hearts – a prolonged trip; emigration.
Nine of Hearts/Three of Diamonds – a stable love affair.

Eight of Diamonds next to any Club – extended travel.
Eight of Diamonds/Eight of Clubs – enduring love.
Eight of Diamonds/Five of Diamonds – a windfall.
Eight of Diamonds/Eight of Hearts – a new job or enterprise.
Eight of Diamonds/Eight of Spades – sickness.

Eight of Hearts/Five of Hearts – an unexpected gift.
Eight of Spades/Seven of Diamonds – insecurity.
Eight of Spades/Five of Spades – a jealous rival.

Seven of Diamonds next to any Club – financial problems.
Seven of Diamonds/Six of Diamonds – beware of speculation.
Seven of Spades next to any Spade court card – treachery.

Three of Diamonds/Two of Clubs – a pleasant surprise.

Preparations

Keeping in mind all the points already made, the next step is to select and lay out the cards. There is a traditional method of doing so and it is a good idea to follow this procedure as it is designed to put the interpreter and enquirer in the right frame of mind for the reading by focusing attention on the matter at hand.

Firstly, the interpreter should shuffle the pack to ensure that the cards are free of any previous influences before placing them on the table. If doing readings for several people in succession, the cards are always shuffled by the interpreter before a new reading is started in order to 'neutralise' them and to allow the reader to disassociate his/her mind from the previous reading.

If a significator is to be used, it is selected at this stage and placed to one side before the rest of the pack is put face down on the table. The enquirer is invited to pick up the cards and shuffle them thoroughly while concentrating on the matter that is uppermost in his mind at the time of the reading. He then places the cards in the centre of the table and with his left hand – literally and figuratively the one closest to the heart – cuts them into three towards the interpreter.

The reader completes the cut by placing the first pile on top of the second and the third on top of that before spreading the cards face downwards across the table with their edges slightly overlapping. Still using his left hand, the enquirer selects the required number of cards (this will vary according to the lay-out used) one by one and hands these to the reader as they are chosen. The interpreter places the selected cards face down in a pile in strict order until the correct number is reached and then removes the surplus cards from the table.

If a significator is to be used, it may be added to the pile now. The easiest way is to fan the selected cards out, making sure they remain face down, and ask the querent to place the significator amongst them wherever he wishes. The cards are now ready to be laid out but, whichever spread is used, it is important to keep them in the order chosen, so they must either be dealt from the bottom or the whole pile turned face up and dealt from the top.

Choosing a spread

The first thing to consider is the purpose of the reading: do you want an overall picture or wish to highlight one particular situation, problem or question? Once this point is clear in your mind, select the spread that seems to fit your requirements best. Some spreads call for as few as seven cards and are, perhaps, most suitable for question solving, others utilise the entire deck; some require the cards to be shuffled, cut and dealt several times, others only once: the variety is practically endless.

With practice, you will probably find that you tend to use one spread in preference to another; you may even develop your own method of laying out the cards for a reading. It doesn't matter which you do; there is, after all, no wrong or right way to lay out the cards, neither is one spread better than another. Like all the predictive arts, much depends on the object of the reading and the personal preferences of the reader.

So, if you do find one particular spread appeals to you more than another, use it because you will give of your best this way. In any case, the choice is so vast that it is impractical to give more than a few examples here as a starting point for those who have not read the cards before. Most are traditional lay-outs that have been in use for at least a century, in some cases much longer, one or two are relatively modern. So, take your pick – the choice is yours!

The magic square

This is a very simple spread but quite a lot of information can be gleaned from it once you are familiar with the way one card relates to another. A significator is selected and placed in the centre of the table before the other nine cards needed are chosen in the usual manner by the querent. These are then laid in three rows of three as shown in the diagram with the last card dealt covering the significator. The cards are then interpreted according to the following:

1   Individuality: personality and state of mind.
2   Outside influences and unexpected factors.
3   Environmental influences: friends, family, home, etc.
4   The querent's hopes and fears in the matter under consideration.
5   Alternatives: opportunities, challenges and so on.
6   The querent's aspirations and beliefs.
7   Negative, opposing or limiting factors.
8   Positive, constructive and helpful influences.
9   Potential: initiative, possibilities.

The cards are interpreted in two directions: the top row presents a general picture of the prevailing atmosphere, the basis of the querent's current position and attitude which are symbolised by the middle row, and the bottom row indicates future possibilities.

Magic square

Reading the rows down: position 1, 4 and 6 show three facets of the enquirer's nature; cards 2, 9 and 7 denote major factors that must be considered before decisions are made; and cards 3, 5 and 8 indicate the opportunities and favourable outcome of the correct choice.

The key to the spread is the central square because this relates to every other and signifies the potential of the enquirer who, surrounded by possibilities, must make the moves.

The Bohemian spread

This is another simple spread but one which does not call for a significator. Seven cards are chosen in the usual manner and laid out in the sequence shown. Again, each card position relates to a specific aspect of the querent's life and this should be borne in mind when interpreting the spread.

1 The querent's home environment and domestic issues – household goods, renovations, removals, etc.
2 Current influences – those factors that relate directly to the questioner's present circumstances, such as hopes and/or worries.
3 Relationships of all kinds – love, friendship, business or romantic partnerships or, of course, rivals, enemies, etc.

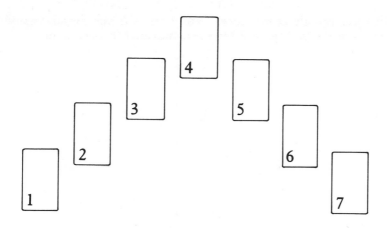

Bohemian spread

4 The querent's eventual wishes in the matter under enquiry – what he/she hopes or wants to achieve.
5 Unexpected assistance or obstacles that are likely to help or hinder the aim signified by the preceding card.
6 Those events that are likely to affect the enquirer's immediate future; probabilities and possibilities.
7 Any helpful influences or fortunate circumstances that the querent can use to his advantage; any chance of good fortune coming his way.

The celestial circle
This nice simple spread is very useful for anyone wanting a good indication of the general trends for the next 12 months. No significator is required, the querent selects 13 cards which are laid out like a clock face, the last card chosen being placed in the centre of the circle.

This card should be interpreted first because it will show the overall emphasis for the coming 12 months. If, for instance, this card is a club, it signifies that the enquirer will be concerned mainly with practical or business matters. A diamond in this position signals that financial affairs or status will be the querent's major concern. A heart augurs well for emotional or romantic interests and a spade denotes a challenging, changeful year ahead.

The other 12 cards are then read in sequence, each representing one month. Card 1 relates to the month in which the reading takes place, irrespective of the date, and is indicative of the overriding influence in the querent's life at that time. Card 2 refers to the calendar month following the reading, card 3 to the month after that and so on.

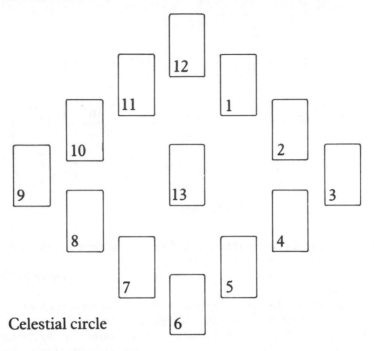

Celestial circle

The wheel of fortune
There are several spreads that involve laying out the cards in a star formation, some using as few as seven cards and others using the entire pack. This one calls for the selection of 21 cards in addition to a centrally placed significator.

This lay-out is sometimes known as the grand star, but I prefer the old title used here because the cards are read as three circles, one inside the other, and in opposing directions – just like the wheel of fortune turning first one way and then the other. The significator acts as the wheel's pivot, around which events turn, and the 21st card, symbolising the eventual outcome or effect on the querent, is placed across the significator.

Contrary to many spreads, the procedure is to interpret the more remote cards first and work inwards towards the significator so that the influences become stronger as the reading progresses. The cards are interpreted in pairs but, before doing this, note any special combinations

or runs (detailed on pages 19-22) in the spread and interpret these first
without disturbing the lay-out.

The pairs are then read, starting with the outer circle and removing
each pair from the spread as they are interpreted. This pairing of the
cards lends a new dimension to the reading, too, because this will in
effect help to highlight any conflicting or complementary factors in the
interpretation. Often, the interpreter will place each pair side by side in
rows at one side of the table so that the sequence can be kept in sight
during the reading (see illustration overleaf).

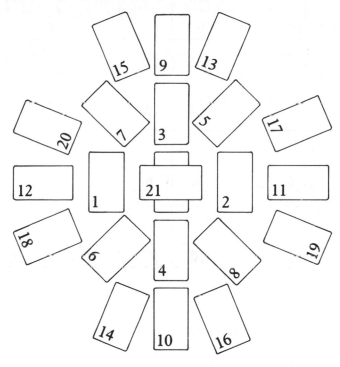

Wheel of fortune

The outer circle is read anti-clockwise: 13 and 15, 20 and 18, 14 and
16, 19 and 17. But with the next circle this procedure is reversed and it is
taken clockwise: 9 and 5, 11 and 8, 10 and 6, 12 and 7. The innermost

ring reverts to the anti-clockwise sequence: 3 and 1, 4 and 2. This leaves the hub of the wheel: the significator crossed by card number 21, the overriding influence or eventual outcome of the matter under consideration.

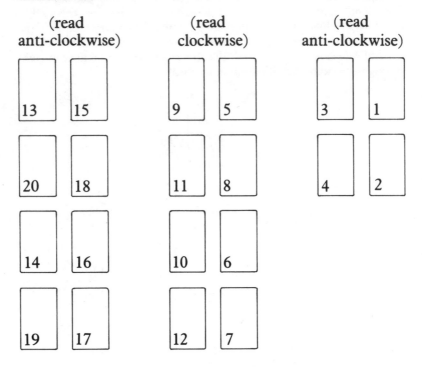

(read anti-clockwise) — 13, 15, 20, 18, 14, 16, 19, 17

(read clockwise) — 9, 5, 11, 8, 10, 6, 12, 7

(read anti-clockwise) — 3, 1, 4, 2

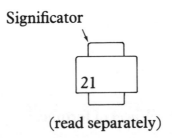

Significator

21

(read separately)

Sequence of pairs (Wheel of fortune)

21-card spread
This is a very simple and popular spread, sometimes referred to as the Romany spread, but its accuracy does depend greatly on the interpreter's knowledge of the individual meanings of the cards and his/her ability to relate one to another. No significator is needed, the 21 cards are dealt out in three rows of seven and read from left to right once any special combinations or runs have been noted and interpreted.

The top row refers to past influences and recent events that have contributed to the present situation.

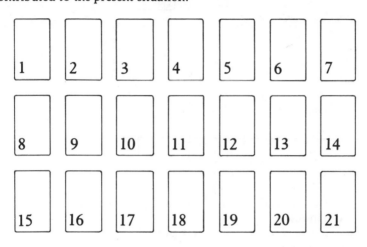

21-Card spread

The middle row represents the querent's present circumstances, current feelings, hopes and wishes in the matter under consideration. It also indicates possible alternatives, opposition and opportunities.

The bottom row denotes the likely future outcome of the current situation.

Each row is interpreted individually according to the cards that fall in it. The overall reading should give a clear indication of the events leading up to the enquirer's present circumstances, the choices that can be made and the probable outcome of these. Some indication of timing can usually be gleaned from the numbered cards on either side of any court cards in the spread.

The pyramid
No significator is required for this spread which is more suitable for considering a specific problem than for a general reading. Select 10 cards

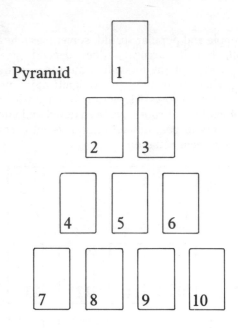

Pyramid

in the usual way and deal these out in the order shown. The cards are then read in rows:

Card number 1, at the apex of the pyramid, represents the overriding aspect or influence.

Cards 2 and 3 indicate the options or alternatives open to the enquirer.

Cards 4, 5 and 6 denote the underlying forces at work which have given rise to the current situation or problem.

The bottom row indicates the best way for the querent to handle the situation or resolve the problem.

The mystic star
As already mentioned, there are several spreads based on a stellar formation and this 8-pointed star calls for the selection of 24 cards in addition to a centrally placed significator. As usual, the significator is chosen by the interpreter and placed face up on the table before the cards are handed to the enquirer to shuffle and cut into three towards the interpreter with his left hand.

At this point, there comes a break with the traditional procedure because, instead of completing the cut, the interpreter turns the three piles over so that the bottom card is uppermost and removes the top card from each heap. These three cards are then placed to one side of the table and the remainder of the pack returned to the querent who reshuffles and cuts the cards in the normal manner before selecting 24 cards.

These are dealt, by the interpreter, in a star formation around the significator in the sequence shown. The cards are interpreted in groups of three, first singly and then in conjunction, starting with the three cards outside the star. These are known as the 'indicators' and will set the tenor of the reading as a whole because they denote a key to the querent's current situation or problem and indicate the overriding influence.

The interpreter next considers the three cards immediately above the significator and reads these before moving round the circle, anti-clockwise, interpreting each group of three cards in combination. Finally, the spread as a whole is considered and summarised within the context of the situation outlined or highlighted by the three indicators.

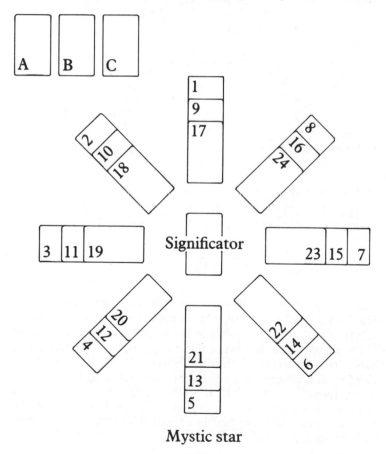

Mystic star

The fan

Another traditional lay-out is the fan shape and, again, there are several variations of this using different numbers of cards. I will, therefore, describe the basic principle and suggest ways to adapt the spread to accommodate more cards.

Firstly, the interpreter decides on a significator but, unlike other spreads mentioned here, this card is not removed from the pack. The querent shuffles, cuts and selects 13 cards in the usual manner, handing these to the interpreter as they are chosen. Without changing their order, the interpreter checks to see whether the significator is among them or, if not, the seven of the same suit which can be used as a substitute.

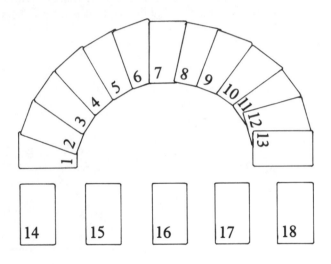

The fan

If neither card is present, the querent reshuffles, cuts and selects 13 cards as before and the interpreter again checks for the significator or its substitute. If neither card appears in the second selection, the reading should be put off to another day as this is regarded as an indication that the cards are not ready to provide an answer.

However, assuming the time to be right, the selected cards are laid out in a fan formation from left to right, with their edges slightly overlapping, as shown in the illustration. The enquirer then selects a further five cards which are laid in a straight row from left to right beneath the fanned cards.

The cards in the fan denote the underlying forces and current influences of the enquirer's situation and are read first. Look for the significator (or seven) and, counting that as card number 1, interpret the fifth card to the right; then, counting that card as number 1, read the fifth card to its right and so on until all the cards in the fan, with the exception of the significator, have been interpreted. This sounds more complicated than it is but, to make the sequence plain, we will assume that card number 2 in the lay-out shown is the significator; the card order for interpretation would be: 6, 10, 1, 5, 9, 13, 4, 8, 12, 3, 7, 11.

Next, the five cards below the fan are interpreted in pairs, starting at either end of the row and working towards the middle. So, cards 14 and 18 are read together, as are 15 and 17, and the centre card, 16, is read on its own. These five cards denote the options and possibilities open to the querent and the likely outcome of the matter under consideration.

This basic lay-out can be adapted to accommodate more cards. The same general principles apply, only the numbers will vary. For instance, the querent can select 17 cards for the fan and a further seven cards for the row below. In such a spread, every seventh card from the significator is read until all the cards in the fan have been interpreted. (Remember, the significator and each subsequent card read is counted as number 1 when counting off the cards to the seventh.) Again, the row below the fan is interpreted in pairs starting at both ends and working inwards – 18 and 24, 19 and 23, 20 and 22 – leaving number 21, in the centre, to be read last.

If you wish to expand the lay-out further, deal 21 cards in the fan with a row of nine cards below. Again, exactly the same method is employed except that every ninth card in the fan is read in sequence from the significator's position.

The mystical cross
This spread calls for a significator which is taken from the pack and placed to one side before the enquirer shuffles, cuts and selects 12 cards in the usual manner. The querent next places the significator anywhere he likes among the cards chosen and the interpreter then lays these out in two rows to form an equal-armed cross as shown in the diagram.

The vertical row is read from top to bottom and refers to the querent's present situation; the horizontal row is read from left to right and relates to those influences that will affect current circumstances. If the significator falls in the vertical row, it indicates that the enquirer is in the grip of circumstances beyond his control but should it fall in the horizontal row, he has the matter in hand.

The fourth card laid, at the centre of the cross, represents the factor around which the whole situation revolves. This card will, therefore, provide the key to the matter under consideration.

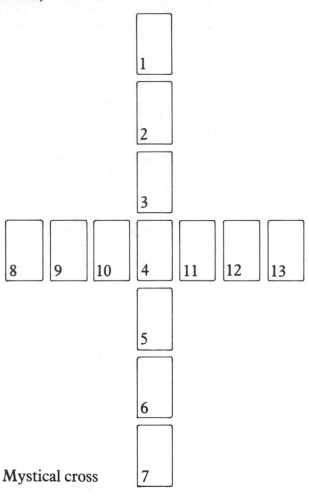

Mystical cross

The horoscope wheel
The querent selects 13 cards in the usual manner. The first 12 are laid out in the same order and positions as the houses in a horoscope and the 13th card selected is placed in the centre of the circle thus formed. Each position is associated with a specific aspect of the querent's life and the cards are interpreted within this context. Here, then, are the traditional meanings of each house/card position:

1   The enquirer: his physical energy, personal ambitions, the image he presents to the outside world and the state of development he has achieved.

2   Material affairs: the querent's actual financial/material status or attitude to money and possessions; also his hopes and wishes in such matters.

3   Communication: education, written agreements, short journeys, day-to-day contacts and chance relationships; also the querent's mental capabilities.

4   The home: the enquirer's personal, private life, place of residence, living conditions, family roots and childhood environment; also property and real estate.

5   Creativity and self-expression: birth, children and their affairs; romance; artistic or creative activities; speculation and new undertakings.

6   Work, health and service to others. The enquirer's actual occupation as well as his attitude towards colleagues, employers and/or employees.

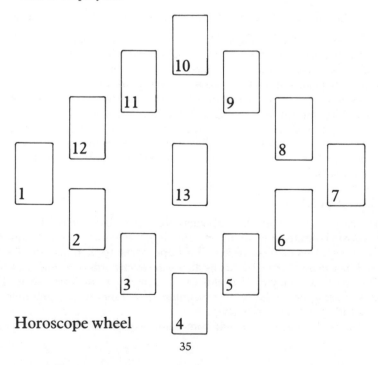

Horoscope wheel

7 Close relationships: love, marriage, business and personal partnerships but not relatives. Also 'open' enemies – litigation, law suits, etc.

8 Wills, legacies and other people's money; big business such as banking, insurance, etc. Also transformation and regeneration: death, rebirth, the occult and the enquirer's attitude to such matters.

9 Spiritual energy; religion, philosophy, the law, further education; morals, conscience, ideals and dreams; foreign people and places, long journeys.

10 The external aspects of life: career, status, reputation. The querent's attitude towards his responsibilities, professional achievements and authority.

11 Social relationships: friends, acquaintances and group activities; pleasures and pastimes. Also the enquirer's hopes and ambitions.

12 The internal aspects of life: fantasies, daydreams, intrigues and fears; secret enemies, limitations, inhibiting factors or karmic responsibilities.

13 The overall influence of the reading: the summator of the spread.

This lay-out can be adapted easily to cover a specific period. Instead of selecting 13 cards only, the whole pack is used. The first 13 are chosen and laid out as previously explained, then the querent selects another 13 which are placed in the same sequence on top of those already laid, and so on. In other words, in position 1 will be the 1st, 14th, 27th and 40th cards laid; in position 2, the 2nd, 15th, 28th and 41st; etc.

The four cards in each 'house' will correspond to a week or a quarter and should be interpreted according to the subject matter relating to that house. In this way, the reading can cover a month or year in the querent's life.

General guidelines

The variety of ways in which playing cards can be laid out for divinatory purposes is limited only by the imagination of the interpreter. However, the ten spreads detailed here will, I hope, serve to demonstrate that a reading can be obtained by using as few as seven cards or as many as 52. The method of laying out the cards is really immaterial, it is the consultant's knowledge of their meanings and ability to interpret them – on all levels – that is important.

This is something that will come with experience, though psychic ability would, of course, help. Don't forget, though, that each card in a spread must be interpreted according to the position in which it falls, the surrounding or opposing cards, the personal circumstances of the enquirer and the nature of the matter under consideration. For example, in the Bohemian spread, position 3 refers to friends, colleagues, partners, etc, but if an adverse card fell here in a spread concerning a business deal, it could equally well relate to rivals, competitors or enemies.

So, it is essential to familiarise yourself with the positive and negative aspects of each card as well as the significance of each position in a spread. One of the easiest methods is to practise interpreting one particular lay-out using different cards each time until you build up confidence and then repeat the exercise using another spread, and so on.

You'll be surprised how quickly you will learn to play your cards right!

Dice

As with many forms of divination, dice reading is a very ancient art practised since at least 2000 BC. The use of dice for this purpose probably evolved from sortilege *(see* glossary).

Early dice were not the same cube shape as we know dice now, the Greeks and Romans used the ankle-bones of sheep; there were long dice, dice with 14 faces and even six-sided figurines. In fact, dice have been known to have up to 20 faces. They can be made from a number of materials including bone, ivory, wood or stone.

The standard western dice has the one spot on the face opposite the six spot, therefore the two spot is opposite the five and the three opposite the four. The modern method of divination using dice is known as astragalomancy and the most common number of dice used is two or a pair. However, three dice can also be used.

As with most things, different people have different beliefs on how to read dice. Old traditions insisted that dice were thrown in silence and that you couldn't throw your own dice, someone else must throw them for you otherwise the answer given would not be correct.

There is a school of thought that still exists today which believes that you should draw a circle approximately 12 inches in diameter on a flat surface, using chalk, then throw your dice. If they all land outside the circle throw them again. If this happens twice it must be taken as a sign that you are not destined to have a reading. Never cast the dice a third time.

If, however, any dice land inside the circle they are added together and an interpretation can be given. A dice outside the circle is an indication that there is a quarrel brewing. If the dice actually falls on the floor during casting there may well be an estrangement. In the unlikely event that the two dice actually fall on top of each other you must refuse a present or gift offered to you as it will turn out to be unfortunate or unlucky for you.

Dice prophecies are said to come true within nine days of being given. If, however, this doesn't happen, the forecast event will not occur at all. As with other forms of divination, you must not consult the dice too often. Many believe that you should not have more than one consultation a week and that it is unlucky to try the dice on Mondays and Wednesdays.

How to consult the dice

If you are using two dice to answer a question (the most common use), place them in a cup then concentrate hard on the question to be asked. When ready, tip the two dice out of the cup into the chalk circle. If one of the dice falls outside the circle it is not counted of course. Just use the number of spots uppermost on the one dice in the circle when consulting the list of answers. If two dice fall inside the circle add the number of spots uppermost on the dice together, then consult the answers.

One spot only means that the answer to your question is yes.

Two spots gives a negative answer.

Three indicates that you will have to take care, but that everything is OK.

Four spots indicates that you need to give much thought and attention to the matter in question before proceeding.

Five spots uppermost is a sign that you are about to have some good luck.

Six is a sign given when it is OK to proceed with whatever it is you want to do.

Seven spots indicate that you should have faith.

Eight that you will have to be patient and bide your time.

Nine spots denote an extremely positive yes to the question posed.

Ten indicates that the situation is doubtful.

Eleven spots can be taken as a rebuke, because your question or problem is nonsense.

Twelve spots indicate that there is a chance that whatever you are asking the dice about will not happen anyway.

Some people find that they get the most accurate readings if they use three dice. This type of divination is not usually used, though, for answering a specific question but to see what can be expected in the near future. However, the same technique of drawing a circle and throwing the dice is used.

This is what you can expect to happen if the following number of spots come up:

If *three* spots appear there may be some good news on its way to you as this number of spots indicates a pleasant surprise.

If *four* spots are seen it is not a good sign because there may be bad news or an unpleasant surprise on its way to you. Four spots often appear when someone is about to have some bad luck too.

If *five* come up it indicates that happiness will come to you, perhaps in an unexpected way and possibly involving a stranger.

When *six* is the total of spots on the three dice you may be unfortunate in a business or financial matter and, as a result, could end up losing money. In addition, this number of spots also implies the loss of something valuable to you.

If *seven* spots appear on your dice, you must exercise extreme caution if you don't want to end up the subject of gossip or scandal.

When *eight* spots appear take it as a sign that the past will catch up with you and you'll be blamed for some misdeed you committed some time ago.

Nine indicates luck in love. Either you or someone close to you will marry – and soon. This marriage will come out of the blue and take everyone quite by surprise. This number of spots may also symbolise the end to a quarrel (possibly a long-term one) as there is likely to be a reconciliation.

When *ten* spots are the total on the dice it is an indication that something new is about to start; this may be a birth or a friendship, or it could refer to a promotion and/or business success.

A total of *eleven* spots implies that there will be a parting of the ways, someone close to you may leave. This number is also a sign of illness or death.

Twelve spots will turn up when you are about to receive some good news which may well arrive in the post. If this good news is a job offer, seek the advice of others before you accept it otherwise you may regret it later.

Many people believe that the number *thirteen* is unlucky and in this case it is true. It indicates that there will be much sorrow and grief on its way to you.

Should *fourteen* spots be the total on the dice it means that a friend will be instrumental in a meeting between you and another person, the result of which will be mutual admiration and a long-lasting relationship.

Fifteen spots are a warning sign, they signify that danger lurks and that if you are not careful you will suddenly become involved in certain activities which are not strictly legal.

A happy and enjoyable journey is foretold when *sixteen* spots appear. This journey need not be abroad, in fact it needn't even be over a long distance.

Seventeen is the sign of a change of plan, perhaps involving someone

41

from overseas, but one which will result in a very profitable business deal.

Should the number *eighteen* appear you have turned up the best possible number of all for it signifies prosperity, happiness and success.

Dominoes

Dominoes are frequently associated with runes when, in fact, they are closer to dice for divination purposes.

The first recording of these tiles is believed to be in the 12th century BC in China. However, dominoes were not as we in the West know them, black with white spots, but white with red spots and there were 32 of them in a set whereas we only have 28.

This form of divination was used extensively in Korea and India and was frequently combined with gambling. So how did dominoes come to Great Britain? Well, they came from China via France and Italy in the 18th century.

Domino readings

The dominoes are usually read by laying them face down and selecting three tiles at random which are then read in conjunction with each other. Obviously the best reading is provided by someone with clairvoyant powers as he/she will do more than just interpret the spots. But you won't know if you have this skill unless you try.

There are of course several variations on the method of choosing the dominoes. You can pick one and reshuffle, pick another, reshuffle, etc; you can lay them face down in four rows and pick three at random; or lay them in squares, circles or oblongs, whatever takes your fancy. Providing you don't draw more than three tiles and don't consult them more than once a week you should get an accurate reading. As with nearly all forms of divination, it is thought that excess use reduces the power of the medium. Some people believe that dominoes must not be consulted on a Monday or Friday but that, of course, is up to you or the reader to decide.

When undertaking a reading the meanings symbolised by the combination and number of spots should be elaborated on by the reader so that it applies to each individual client.

The following is an outline of the meanings of each tile but it will vary slightly depending on the other two dominoes picked.

43

A six-six tile

When the tile bearing the combination of six spots either side is drawn the drawer will have much joy, success and happiness in everything that he/she does: in fact this is considered to be the best domino of all. It is also a warning to farmers that they may have to sell land to make ends meet.

A six-five tile

This combination of pips indicates that you will go up in someone's estimation because you have performed a kind act. This doesn't mean that you will be going around just waiting to perform this good deed. In fact in most cases you won't even realise you have done it until it is pointed out to you later.

This domino symbolises close friendship and is the tile of a benefactor. So something good may be coming your way but it won't be as quickly as you thought – so be patient. A six-five domino can also indicate that you must persevere with whatever project you are presently working on. Those who choose this tile will have luck in love.

A six-four tile

This is not one of the best tiles to pick – but then it's not one of the worst either and you may learn something about yourself and other people along the way. A six-four domino indicates that there will be a disagreement which in some instances may lead to a court case. Unfortunately, the outcome may not be favourable. This unfortunate situation will, however, draw you closer to someone in a romantic sense and may even result in a quick marriage.

A six-three tile

There are several interpretations to be gained from this domino, so the reader must ascertain which is the correct one – but that's the art of undertaking a reading and not everyone can do it! A six-three combination indicates that you are going to travel on holiday and have a really smashing time, with good weather, nice things to eat and pleasant company. This doesn't necessarily have to be abroad though.

On the other hand, it can also mean that you are going to travel or undertake a journey that will change your whole life – possibly emigration or a job abroad.

The third interpretation for this domino is that you may receive a gift while travelling, though not necessarily of the material kind. This tile is considered to be lucky for lovers of all ages. For married couples it signifies a long and fruitful union.

A six-two tile
This will be chosen by someone who has an improvement in circumstances on the way. This will probably come about as a result of some good luck heading your way, possibly concerning a business venture. However, it is only lucky for honest folk, dishonesty will not succeed. Thrift and hard work are the order of the day.

A six-one tile
Ring those church bells, a wedding is foretold by this tile. It also indicates that there will be an end soon to at least one of your problems involving a close friend. For married people it indicates good fortune in middle life. You will, though, have to learn to let go of your children when the time comes.

A six-blank tile
This is not a particularly pleasant domino but, provided that you are alert, you may be able to stave off its effects. Avoid people who appear to be false or deceitful because when this tile appears it's very likely that they are just what they seem.

There may also be some gossip circulating, so watch how you behave or it could be about you! This domino may also signify a death in the family or in your immediate circle of friends.

A five-five tile
All change – this domino implies that you will be making changes and for the better. You may change jobs or move house or in some cases do both; whatever the case, the outcome will be most beneficial. This tile will also turn up in the three chosen by someone who is about to break away and start a new career in a completely different field. But don't worry, the outcome is likely to be very lucrative.

A five-four tile
The tile of surprise, a five-four domino indicates good fortune. This will be of the material kind although you won't be able to create it yourself; in other words, this is not the time for speculation or investment. Your money will come unexpectedly, possibly as a windfall, bonus or tax rebate. It may also come as an unexpected job offer from someone who can provide better terms than you have at present.

Whatever its method of arrival, you'll just have to sit back and wait for the benefits to come to you. Young ladies who choose this domino had better find themselves a good career for they are likely to fall in love with a man who doesn't earn much – but, as the saying goes, love conquers all.

A five-three tile

This is a pleasing tile to choose because it indicates that everything in your life at present is running along smoothly. There should be a pleasant atmosphere at home and at work, with other people happy to give you any advice and assistance that you need, whenever you need it. There could be some good news on its way to you, perhaps brought by a visitor. For young couples this domino indicates financial security for a number of years.

A five-two tile

The five-two combination is frequently the omen of a birth. This may not directly involve the person who has chosen the tile and may refer to someone else in the family or a very close friend. The tolerance and patience of someone close to you will make you stop and take a closer look at yourself, possibly causing you to make conscious changes to your nature. This is not a very favourable tile for marriage because it indicates many difficulties and disagreements.

A five-one tile

This domino will be drawn by someone who is about to have a fabulous year socially; there will be plenty of invitations coming your way and for many different kinds of events too. So, make the most of this opportunity to widen your circle of friends and make useful contacts.

However, take care in financial dealings as there may be a major disappointment in this area. For those who are married this domino indicates an addition to the family – not necessarily a baby.

A five-blank tile

Whoever chooses this tile will have to be on guard at all times. If drawn by a woman it indicates that she will have to keep a close and watchful eye on her budgeting otherwise she could be in serious trouble, with essential services being cut off and the cupboard bare too!

Should a male draw this domino it denotes that he will have to learn to curb his selfishness, imprudence and urge to gamble or he may end up on the losing side of life. This domino frequently appears when a friend needs comforting, but take care what you say in this stressful situation otherwise you could end up doing irreparable damage.

A four-four tile

This is a rather mixed domino to pick because it depends on your job whether it is favourable or not. For those who are artistic, creative or who work out of doors – in whatever field – it is a good sign. Work will progress very well, in fact in many cases better even than your wildest dreams.

However, those who rely on their mental abilities in their jobs may run into difficulties and delays which hinder and prevent them from reaching their goals. A four-four tile can also signify fun events such as parties and celebrations – possibly a wedding.

A four-three tile
If you pick this domino as one of your three, you can expect to marry when you are young. You may have only one child but that will probably be your own choice. People who turn up this tile may be expecting problems in their lives but should not worry because these will not materialise. Your life-style should be comfortable too, so what more could you want?

A four-two tile
For many this will be a fortunate domino because it indicates changes. These may be in your career, love life or financial situation. In most instances these changes will be for the better, but for a few people they may not. This domino also indicates losses through misfortune, death or robbery. Someone you have trusted in the past may not turn out to be worthy of that trust, so take care.

A four-one tile
Pay off your financial debts as quickly as you can because this tile predicts financial difficulties ahead. However, it is not all gloom and doom as anyone drawing this domino will have a blissfully happy marriage and a large number of children as a result. (Possibly the cause of financial hardship!) There will be much happiness for this person, though.

A four-blank tile
This tile unfortunately predicts disappointment in love. Whether male or female, and no matter how many times the questioner is engaged, he/she will not marry. If you have a secret and this tile comes up, don't tell it to anyone, keep it to yourself or you will end up in trouble.

If you are pregnant this domino indicates that you are in for a surprise because it predicts that you are going to have twins or triplets. If you are doing a reading for someone else and this domino turns up try to be careful how you convey this news or she may go into labour on the spot!

A three-three tile
This is a very fortunate tile, it indicates great financial wealth. You may gain this wealth through a number of avenues – but whatever the case, the money will just keep rolling in.

A three-two tile

What a good domino to pick – as long as you are not pregnant, that is. If you are, you should take care of your health and do as you are instructed by those who know.

A three-two tile indicates a good and happy marriage, with no financial worries. You may also benefit greatly from travel. Careful investment is favoured when this tile appears, but don't make wild speculations because these won't work out.

A three-one tile

This is an unfortunate tile to choose although, with care, most of its harmful influences can be staved off. There may be scandal, unpleasant rumours or gossip floating about and if you don't heed this warning it may be about you! A three-one tile also warns of a lawsuit, so watch what you say about others too.

A three-blank tile

A domino with only three dots on one side indicates quarrels, disagreements and full-blown arguments. If it appears in a man's reading, he must choose his lady carefully (that is if it's not too late already) otherwise he will land himself with someone of a tempermental disposition.

For the ladies, it is a sign that her man may be rather foolish with a tendency to get involved in fights. If this tile appears when you are going to a party, try to avoid those who are likely to provoke you.

A two-two tile

Business success is predicted by this domino, although this will not lead to great wealth, just financial contentment. Home life will be very good, too, with children adding to your happiness.

A two-one tile

This domino is frequently turned up by young females and predicts that they will marry young, probably to someone with a lot of money. This may not turn out well though for they may be widowed at a young age, too. Most young ladies will remarry and have a long and happy union. Should a man turn up this domino it indicates that he will suffer financial loss through business dealings.

A two-blank tile

This is a domino of mixed fortunes. For travel or a journey it bodes well, all will go smoothly and you may even meet someone of interest en route. For those with dealings that are less than honest, they will do well too; but for anyone who is upstanding and law-abiding this tile indicates poverty – there's no justice in this world.

Should this tile appear in a young man's selection it denotes that he will have disappointments in his career. In an older lady's choice, it indicates that she will have problems getting her partner to earn an honest living.

A one-one tile
Anyone who turns up a double ace is probably worried about a problem but shouldn't be because it will solve itself. This is a very fortunate tile to pick as it indicates much happiness in all aspects of life.

A one-blank tile
If you turn up this domino prepare yourself for a visitor. This person may be a total stranger who brings interesting news, possibly concerning finance. Don't take every word he/she says as gospel, though, check out the facts before getting too carried away.

A blank-blank tile
This is considered to be the worst tile of all. It indicates misfortune and disappointment in all aspects of life, loss of status, money, difficulties in love – the list is endless. However, if you are involved in fraudulent activities, you are likely to prosper.

Numerology

An introduction

As with most occult subjects, everyone seems to have their own ideas and opinions about the origins of numerology and how best to undertake readings, so I suppose I'm no exception! What one must bear in mind, though, is that with these sorts of subjects there is no correct or incorrect way to practise a particular art.

Numerology, numeromancy, gematria or arithmancy have not always been the names given to the study of numbers. These are relatively modern terms for this ancient method of divination. Nevertheless, the significance of numbers has played quite a strong part in people's lives for thousands and thousands of years, dating back to prehistoric times, in fact, when mankind is said to have been able to count and work with some sort of numbering system.

The Babylonians and the ancient Egyptians also had their theories about numbers and their significance. Many people considered that numbers had and in some cases still have occult significance especially those interested in the Kabala. But the man that everyone thinks of when talking about numerical theories is, of course, Pythagoras.

Pythagoras was a Greek born in about 580 BC, he was a philosopher, mathematician, astronomer and astrologer who, it is said, was extremely well travelled. One of the many places he visited in the course of his studies was Egypt and, as any mathematician will tell you, the Egyptians must have had some understanding of numbers and mathematics in order to build pyramids.

Pythagoras formed the theory that everything could be expressed in terms of numbers. He thought that man could understand and comprehend the universe a little easier if everything was put in numerical form; for example, the four elements: earth, fire, air and water.

A Pythagorean school was initiated to study the complexity of numbers and the whole science surrounding this subject.

The Fellowship Order for Esoteric Study of Numbers was a secretive organisation with strict rules about passing on their teachings. However, as with most organizations, there were leaks. Members felt that their knowledge and theories should be shared with others.

Pythagoreans believed, as Pythagoras himself did, that numbers had personality or character and that certain numbers were therefore stronger than others. Odd numbers were considered to be more powerful than even ones; also, odd numbers were thought to be masculine and even numbers to be feminine.

As with most subjects, numerology has developed and evolved over the years and the many forms practised today are quite different to those of Pythagoras' time.

Many, many books have been published about numerology, not just recently either, because this is considered to be one of the easiest occult subjects to learn and master. Those who have and who are still studying numerology will probably dispute this fact for they will tell you that it is constantly developing and changing as time goes on. They will also tell you that there is no single person alive who knows everything there is to know about numerology. Many know a lot but not all!

However, it is a well-known theory that each one of us has a lucky and an unlucky number and certain races believe particular numbers to be unlucky and others lucky by definition. For example, it is said that when asked to choose a number, a German will nearly always pick 5, whereas the British usually choose 2, 3 or 7. No one really knows why.

The best way to discover your own lucky number is to write down the dates of major happy events in your life, the numbers of houses you have lived in, etc, and see if one number keeps cropping up. If so, you can consider that to be a lucky number for you. If you want to know your unlucky number, employ the same process for unfortunate events.

Letters to numbers

There are many different systems of calculating your character or name number. However, whichever method is used, the basic principle is the same: each letter of the alphabet is given a numerical value.

Some people find that they get the most accurate result by calculating their name number from their christian name only. Others prefer to use both surname and christian name or names, it is all a matter of personal choice. The best way to check the accuracy of your character or name number is to work it out using all the different combinations and methods, then check the character traits described for each number on page 54.

If you are known by a shortened version of your full name, for example Ali instead of Alison, calculate your name number using that. The same advice applies if you are known by a nickname.

The unit system for converting letters to numbers uses only the numbers from 1 to 9 and their planetary vibrations.

All letters comprising the number 1 are influenced by the positive aspects of the Sun; 2 by the negative influence of the Moon; 3 by Jupiter; 4 by the negative influence of the Sun; 5 by Mercury; 6 by Venus; 7 by the positive influences of the Moon; 8 by Saturn; and 9 by Mars.

The letters and their corresponding numbers are:

A B C D E F G H I J K L M N O P Q R S T U V W X Y Z
1 2 2 4 5 8 3 8 1 1 2 3 4 5 7 8 1 2 3 4 6 6 6 7 1 7

There are also three combinations of letters which have their own value of 9, these are: Th, Ts, Tz.

The Hebrew Kabalistic system of converting letters to numbers is rather different as up to 22 numbers are used. As Hebrew is not our everyday language, I have not included the Hebrew letters here, only the English equivalents and their planetary or zodiacal vibrations.

All letters with the number 1 are influenced by Mercury; 2 by Virgo; 3 by Libra; 4 by Scorpio; 5 by Jupiter; 6 by Venus; 7 by Sagittarius; 8 by Capricorn; 9 by Aquarius; 10 by Uranus; 11 by Neptune; 12 by Pisces; 13 by Aries; 14 by Taurus; 15 by Saturn; 16 by Mars; 17 by Gemini; 18 by Cancer; 19 by Leo; 20 by the Moon; 21 by the Sun; and 22 by the Earth.

The letters and their corresponding numbers are:

A B C D E F G H I J K L M N O P Q R S T U V W X Y Z
1 2 11 4 5 17 3 3 8 10 10 12 13 14 16 17 19 20 21 22 5 5 5 15 10 7

There are also three combinations of letters which have their own value, they are:　　　Th　　　Ts　　　Tz
　　　　　　　　　9　　　18　　　18

The easiest method for converting letters to numbers is the simplified, modern Pythagorean system. This uses numbers from 1 to 9. Again, planetary influences or ruling planets are important.

All letters with the number 1 are influenced by the Sun; 2 by the New Moon; 3 by Jupiter; 4 by the Sun and Uranus; 5 by Mercury; 6 by Venus; 7 by Neptune and the Full Moon; 8 by Saturn; and 9 by Mars.

The letters and their corresponding numbers are:

A B C D E F G H I J K L M N O P Q R S T U V W X Y Z
1 2 3 4 5 6 7 8 9 1 2 3 4 5 6 7 8 9 1 2 3 4 5 6 7 8

Once you have chosen whichever method appeals to you most, you can continue. I am going to use the simple Pythagorean system here.

Calculating your character or name number is quite simple. Take a clean sheet of paper, space out your letters and write the name in question on it clearly. Beneath each letter write the numerical value given in the chosen system (this is why the letters need to be spread out).

For example: A L I S O N   T A Y L O R

            1 3 9 1 6 5   2 1 7 3 6 9

$$= 25 \qquad\qquad = 28$$

$$25 + 28 = 53 \qquad 5 + 3 = 8$$

Therefore, Alison's character or name number is 8. Once you have worked out your number you are ready to look up its significance on the following pages.

Birth or character numbers

Number 1

This number cannot be divided into any other number and is therefore considered to be a complete or whole number. It is often associated with God, a supreme power or the Sun.

Those whose birth number is 1 are usually natural leaders, those who stand out in a crowd and tend to take over the command of groups with the maximum of ease. If this is your number, you are independent and possess a strong, in some cases too strong, forceful character but are a wonderful organiser.

You would prefer to work alone, and at the top of your chosen career – this is probably just as well as you tend to judge others by your own very high standards. At times you may also become rather ruthless and stubborn in the pursuit of your aims and ambitions. But, as the saying goes, 'be nice to those you meet on the way up as you may meet them on the way back down.'

Relax a little and stop being so competitive in everything you do because you will then make new friends and have a lot more fun.

Number 2

Number 2 is the first feminine number, therefore you should have a gentle, passive nature. You are courteous and enjoy, in some cases need, people around you as you have a tendency to become lonely when left on your own.

Number 2 folk make excellent right-hand or back-up people because they need the mental stimulation of others and don't really want to work solely on their own: co-operation is the keyword.

In both the home and working environment, you are dependable, warm, sympathetic and understanding, which makes you a pleasure to be with. However, because you are such a good listener others tend to burden you with their problems. So, you should learn to speak out for yourself when you have a problem and make others listen to you for a change.

As you are such a sensitive creature you may be rather prone to depression and or bouts of moodiness. Care must be taken to control this trait otherwise it will cause problems at work and a loss of friends in your social life.

Number 3
Number 3 is the first proper masculine number; it is also the number of the past, present and future.

Those who have this as their birth number tend to be conscientious and ambitious but are inclined to grow tired and bored quickly if saddled with routine work. You most enjoy being mentally stimulated by constant change and challenges in all areas of your life. But you are a born worrier under that carefree, optimistic and happy-go-lucky image that you put on for the public.

You proud people are rather reluctant to be under an obligation to anyone else and for this reason are inclined to avoid any form of commitment in all areas of life.

Number 3 people are fortunate, though, because they possess some of the characteristics of both the number 1 and number 2 groups. You can give and take orders quite happily and are therefore likely to rise quickly in your chosen career, provided of course that you don't get bored first!

Adaptability is one of your greatest assets and you should make full use of this at work in order to advance your career but, whatever happens, you are lucky and will enjoy a prosperous life.

Number 4
Number 4 people are not as straightforward in character as those in groups 1, 2 or 3. There are two quite different sides to your personality. On the surface you appear practical and hardworking but rather reserved in manner; however, under your pleasant exterior lurks a rebel. So, if you are provoked you will quickly shed that outer coat and reveal the real you: someone who is more than capable of standing up for him/herself. During your lifetime it is important for you to learn how to master your extremely quick temper, therefore.

Though not motivated by money or the ambition to be the best, you will steadily rise in your chosen career through sheer hard work and the amazing ability that you have of seeing a project through to the end. You are also a great organiser and should make the most of this asset both at home and at work.

You may not always find it easy to form friendships but, once you have, will be an extremely loyal ally who will defend your friends to the bitter end.

Money is frequently left to people with the number 4 and this usually takes the form of a legacy.

Number 5

Those whose birth number is 5 are people of change who have an extremely active, some would say overactive mind. Your aim in life appears to be to cram as many different experiences as possible into your time on earth.

One of the more infuriating habits that you have is the way you constantly change your mind and opinions – at times others find it almost impossible to even keep up with you. New ideas, facts and figures seem to act like a drug to you.

Number 5 people are lively and fun to have around, though. You tend to be optimistic and often enjoy having a little flutter. In fact, you are so adventurous that your motto should be 'I'll try anything once.' Unfortunately, number 5 people can be highly-strung and are rather prone to nerves; so bear this in mind as you dash off on your next adventure.

One of your favourite pastimes is meeting people and travel. It might, therefore, be a good idea to combine these activities in your career, especially as you have the ability to learn quickly, retain facts easily and do not really wish to have a mundane 9 to 5 job.

Number 6

If your birth number is 6 you will possess a strong desire to be needed and appreciated both at work and at home. However, this trait must be watched otherwise you may turn into someone who constantly seeks the approval of others and this can be a very irritating habit.

You are very reliable and trustworthy but can occasionally become rather obstinate over points of principle. You seem to have a natural talent for befriending all sorts of people but must take care that they don't take advantage of you.

To number 6 people home life is very important, so you will try to make your surroundings homely and comfortable whether you live in a large mansion or a tiny bed-sit. Harmony with others is also important to you; therefore you should try to surround yourself with people who are on your own wavelength.

Careers that allow you to work with and help others are likely to give you greatest job satisfaction. You also have strong creative and artistic talents which will help you to advance in your job or career.

Number 7

Your principles are hard to define because you demand and frequently get total freedom and independence in all areas of your life.

This number is often considered to have occult significance. People who are born under its influence frequently have strong spiritual or philosophical beliefs and many of them are intuitive or, in some cases, even psychic.

Number 7 people like you must take care that they don't take their desire for independence and freedom to such extremes that they spend long periods of time on their own and, as a result, become introverted and antisocial. You are hard to get to know because you try to keep the rest of us at arm's length and try to avoid emotional involvement whenever possible. Many number 7 people either have several marriages and divorces or never marry at all.

You may suffer from restlessness and a strong desire to travel; a need that can be fulfilled if you manage to incorporate travel into your job or career.

Number 8

If you are a number 8 person you are likely to have much success in your business life. You have the ability to work hard and industriously but tend to be rather conservative in your attitudes. So you may have difficulty in taking up new ideas or putting new systems into operation.

Although you won't intentionally hurt anyone in your rise up the ladder of success, you do, unfortunately, tend to upset people by your cold manner. However, this is not the true you, under that chilly exterior is someone who has deep and intense feelings and who is often misunderstood by others. Try to relax a bit and be more tolerant of those who do not have your abilities.

Number 8 people often hold wonderful social events as they never do things on a small scale even when they are a bit hard up, which isn't often. Most of you in this group will always have a little spare cash for the pleasures of life.

The number 8 is often associated with worldly success but it can also be the number of sorrow.

Number 9

Those whose birth number is 9 tend to be energetic, active people who are generous not only with their money but with their time and energy. You would love the whole world if this were possible and because of this love of humanity you are likely to be interested if not involved in the Third World and all its problems. Many of this group are strongly attracted to other people's cultures and religions, so may well belong to one of the less common religious cults or groups.

Number 9 people must take care that they do not try to carry the burden of all the world's troubles on their shoulders. There is also a danger that you may become over critical of others and rather cynical of their efforts.

Try to involve yourself in your immediate community as you will discover that your talent for organisation and co-operation can benefit people closer to home than the Third World: a fact that is unlikely to go unnoticed or unappreciated.

Your dynamic talents will allow you to follow any career you choose but it won't all be plain sailing, sometimes you will have to fight to reach your goals in life.

For those who are using the Hebrew Kabala system of calculation, I have included the birth or character numbers up to 22. These are also sometimes referred to as secondary numbers.

Number 10

Those whose birth number is 10 tend to be intellectual, they are often the scatterbrained, professor types. Yet they are very capable of advancing far up the career ladder – providing, that is, that they don't step on other people's toes! You hold strong views about certain subjects and don't much care for anyone who you consider to be wrong or trying to force his/her point of view on you. Try to learn to be more tolerant of those who hold different views or who are not on your intellectual level.

You will strongly desire routine and security in your home life. You are kind and generous to your family but may not always remember birthdays, wedding anniversaries or that you have guests for dinner and must leave work early; your intentions are good though.

For many number 10 people, life will be strongly influenced by fate – this will work out well for some but not for others.

Number 11

Number 11 is a feminine number and is frequently associated with psychic forces and spiritual power. Therefore many people whose birth number is 11 have psychic abilities. They may not discover this talent for many years but nevertheless it's there, waiting to be developed.

You may not be very ambitious as far as work is concerned but will have a strong desire to help others. You get along famously with people and will feel most at home when working or socialising in a group.

On the social scene, you will derive much pleasure from belonging to clubs or societies which are comprised of people who are on your wavelength and can help you develop your talents to the full.

As this is a feminine number you tend to exhibit certain feminine characteristics and therefore are a wonderful peace-maker although you must learn to control your racing mind and stop flitting from one topic to another. Put your active brain to a good use and don't let it draw you into any scheme that is not perfectly legal and above-board.

Number 12

The number 12 is an emotional number which means that those with this as their birth number will have a deep understanding of and sympathy for all human suffering.

Due mainly to their understanding natures, number 12 people have a remarkable capacity for making sacrifices. But you must take care because others tend to find it easy to ill-treat or abuse you. So, try standing up for yourself occasionally and see what happens!

Your ability to offer great warmth and friendship to all sorts of people means that you should never be lonely or on your own for any length of time.

If you are to succeed in a career you must choose carefully and dedicate much of your time to study because you will find this both beneficial and fulfilling.

You need not spend all your life being dominated by others and will discover you can be just as bossy and pushy if you want to be.

A teaching job of some sort may suddenly be offered to people in this group – have a go, if you don't like it you can always give it up.

Number 13

Number 13 is usually associated with ill-fortune but this is not necessarily true. People with this character number are no less or more unlucky than anyone else. Most numerologists who use the Hebrew Kabala (though that's not many) feel that this is the number of a new cycle.

You should be free from problems concerning material and financial cares. You will have the ability to earn a reasonable salary or wage, at least enough to support you and your family as well as giving you a few luxuries.

Number 13 people reap what they sow, so if you put a lot of effort into your work and home life you will get much back in return.

For most people this is a happy number promising long and happy marriage, partnership and children to complete this rosy picture. However, you must not become complacent – spare a thought sometimes for those who are not as well off as you. This need not just be the people of the Third World, there are plenty of people in your own community who could do with some assistance, whether of a financial or practical nature.

Number 14
The number 14 is a material and physical number, so those with this as their birth number will be very interested in the forces of nature and in nature itself.

You have a great affinity with animals and would be well advised to involve them in your working life. You are a steady worker but may sometimes be described as a plodder.

As the number 14 is influenced by the zodiacal sign of Taurus many of you will possess an obstinate or stubborn streak in your nature. You will, however, be a faithful and loyal friend to those whom you have offered friendship.

Number 14 people are sometimes said to be rather dull folk but this is not really true. You may not sparkle as much or be as quick as people in other groups – but that doesn't make you dull, just steady and reliable. You may not come up with great or inspirational ideals, either, but you will be a pillar of society.

Most of you make smashing mums or dads even though you have strict ideas about bringing up children.

Number 15
Number 15 is one of the blacker numbers as it is associated with fate and Karma. It is the number of mystery and so is frequently linked with the underworld and the seamier side of life.

If this is your birth number, you can expect to reap what you sow. Therefore, if you are involved in some sort of activity that is not legal, above-board or is unkind to others, you can expect to pay for this – and not necessarily in this world either.

People who have this birth number tend to have strong and forceful personalities but should learn not to abuse any authority that they do manage to achieve or run the danger of losing what they have gained.

Not everything about you is bad, of course. For instance, if you decide to take someone under your wing you can be very kind and protective towards them.

You will make a good husband or wife, very passionate, and will enjoy a long and rewarding relationship providing that your partner doesn't mind being dominated or bossed about a bit because you can be quite a tyrant at times.

Number 16

Number 16 is another powerful number. You are strongly influenced by your emotional feelings and so are prone to fits of blind anger or temper but, providing you channel this energy into useful activities or competitive events, much good can be achieved.

You are a very passionate person who tends to do things on impulse. This trait means you are an exciting lover as your partner will never know quite what to expect next! You enjoy having a steady relationship but must learn not to get mad at those you love – well, not too often anyway.

At work you will want to be your own boss as you don't much care for taking orders from others. You make a good boss however because you are able to delegate and are fair to everyone. But your staff should take note that you do not suffer fools gladly because they are likely to get a lashing from your sharp tongue if they make silly mistakes.

In your spare or leisure time it might be a good idea if you take up a martial art or some kind of sport where you can combine keeping fit with getting rid of pent-up aggression.

Number 17

For those with the birth number of 17, you are likely to have many love affairs and, in fact, some of you may even have several marriages in the course of life.

You have a strong desire for variety and change in your relationships, so must learn to be discreet in your associations otherwise you will get an unfavourable reputation.

People with this birth number tend to be rather flighty – a trait that may affect both your social and working life. You get bored very quickly and therefore need a job or career that can provide a constant flow of people for you to meet, also something that is not too routine or mundane. A job working for an airline would suit you admirably because it is quite possible that you will meet at least one of your partners while travelling!

Try not to be influenced so strongly by others: if you don't want to do what they want, say so – after all, you can always find yourself a new partner, flatmate or friend.

Number 18

The number 18 indicates that you have a definite wish for a secure domestic life and therefore have a strong attraction to marriage. But you must try to take your time and choose your partner carefully – don't marry the first person that comes along or you will regret it later.

Your partner must hold the same strong views about marriage as you do and should suit you temperamentally, otherwise upsets and arguments are likely to occur periodically. You will put much into your marriage and will expect the same from your partner.

A fair minded individual, you are slow to anger, but that doesn't mean that your temper won't flare up if you are provoked. This characteristic won't be seen often, though, so is likely to surprise others when it does appear.

At work you must try to show that you are not a doormat type. If you disagree with something be brave, stand on your soapbox and say so. You may be surprised at the result – providing you don't do it too often, of course.

You are not likely to reach the top of your chosen career, though, as you are neither ruthless or competitive enough.

Number 19
As your zodiacal influence is Leo, those with the birth number of 19 are naturally ambitious and competitive, so you probably want to be number 1 or the best.

You are quick of mind and find decision-making comes automatically to you, so you are likely to make good headway and progress in your career.

People are very attracted by your magnetic personality. Also, you make a loyal and faithful friend who will freely admit when you have made a mistake about something or have misjudged someone.

You must try to learn to control your hasty and passionate impulses, though, if you wish to avoid setbacks and downfalls. If either of these unfortunate events does occur, however, you do seem to have an amazing ability to bounce right back and learn from your mistakes.

In your leisure time try to join groups or societies that will benefit from your leadership qualities – but do try to refrain from taking them over completely if you can!

Number 20
As people with the birth number of 20 are influenced by the Moon, your life will seem to ebb and flow just like the phases of the Moon.

Sometimes you will be full of ideas, energy and enthusiasm but on other occasions can be very lazy, lacking in energy and feel bored by everything.

There is no way you can overcome these moody traits in your character, however. So you will just have to use them as best you can.

When you are full of power – rush about, do as much as you can but don't agree to any long-term projects because you may run out of steam before you get around to completing them.

When you are low on power, spend some of your time looking at yourself and your surroundings. If you can summon up enough energy, write down the things you see so that you can make changes when you are feeling more dynamic.

Unless you work for yourself, you are not likely to get to the top of your career – but perhaps that's because you don't want to really in any case.

Number 21

Those who have a 21 birth number will always gravitate towards positions of authority and, provided this is handled in the right way, will gain the admiration of others. If you use power to your own advantage and the disadvantage of others, though, it will make you many enemies, who will hold grudges against you for many years to come.

Those with this birth number should be generally healthy but are rather prone to nervous complaints caused mainly through financial worries. So perhaps it would be a good idea to tuck away a nest-egg for a rainy day, just in case!

Number 21 people are attracted by children and in fact children find them fascinating, too. You will make a wonderful father or mother but will be authoritative in your attitude towards their upbringing.

In your spare time you are likely to gain much pleasure from creative activities because under what may appear to be a rather stern exterior is a frustrated artist just waiting to burst out and create.

Number 22

As the Earth is your planetary influence, the season of your birth will determine what sort of character you are.

Those born in the spring will be adventurous and enterprising. Your life's lesson will be to learn how to handle your affairs and gain from them.

If born in the summer months, you have a natural ability to organise and will therefore rise in your chosen career rapidly. But learn how to take knocks in your stride otherwise you will spend much time licking your wounds.

If your number is 22 and you were born in the autumn, you will have a strong desire for companionship. Try to be a bit more independent, though, and stop worrying about what other people think of you.

You will at times be lonely if you were born in the winter months. The first half of your life may be hard but you will learn much and should be able to go on to achieve many of your aims and ambitions in the second half of your life.

Romance numbers

To discover your romance number, take all of your christian or forenames, write them on a clean sheet of paper and give them their numerical values from the system you have chosen to use. Add the numbers up as shown on p. 54; the total will give you your romance number.

Number 1

If your total is 1, you will be attracted by intellectual types. You probably desire variety in your love affairs and therefore may have difficulty in maintaining a steady relationship with one person. Many of you will meet the love of your life at an educational event or somewhere connected with intellectual activities.

Once you are married, hard work will be necessary to make this relationship work. An absence of warmth and affection may lead to a certain amount of bitterness but this can be overcome.

Number 2

A romance number of 2 indicates that you will want to be with a steady partner very much. This doesn't mean that you will take up with the first person who comes along, however; you won't, you are choosey. People in this group tend to be attracted to those who are bright and generous with their affection. Unfortunately, though, your relationships may suffer from criticism or petty disagreement, either within the relationship itself or from a friend or relative.

Number 3

People with the romance number 3 have a strong wish to marry and in some instances may even become idealistic about this state of affairs. But, providing you are able to come back down to earth when the question is popped and view the situation from all sides, all will turn out well in the end. You may discover that you tend always to be attracted to a certain type of the opposite sex; this is not necessarily a bad thing provided you don't fall for those who give you a hard or unpleasant time.

Number 4

People with the romance number 4 are rather prone to becoming jealous and possessive of their chosen partners. You are most likely to be attracted to people who have the ability to stand up for themselves but you must learn to appreciate that not everyone is waiting to snatch your partner away from you at the earliest opportunity. If male, you are probably physically attracted to strong but feminine females; and the ladies will find strong, courageous men attract them.

Number 5

Romance number 5 is very good as it indicates that much will be gained by a steady relationship which leads to marriage. If this is your number you are likely to benefit from the help of your partner, both with regard to your chosen profession and to your financial situation. You may meet the love of your life through religious or philosophical channels, possibly at an event connected with either of these interests or, perhaps, one of you may work in this area.

Number 6

Oh dear! The romance number 6 is not one of the best. Anyone with this number is rather likely to form sudden attachments and this type of impulsive union does not always work out for the best. Your strong desire for companionship, love and affection can, if not watched carefully, cloud your judgement when choosing a partner. Sexual temptations are also a problem to those who belong to this group and may, indeed, lead to separation from your partner, whether married or not.

Number 7

The number 7 usually indicates that the subject will have several partners before marriage. One of these earlier relationships will be serious but may be terminated when one of the partners travels and doesn't return to fulfil promises. This romance number also signifies that you will marry twice. One of your marriage partners is likely to have interests in sports, the outdoor life or travel, so this may be how you meet.

Number 8

A romance number of 8 indicates that you may marry someone older than yourself and not just a few years older either. If this is the case, you will need to take care of your partner's health and understand that he/she may not always be able to keep up with you sexually. You and your chosen mate will help each other greatly in business and social affairs. Sincerity is an important asset to you, so you will be attracted to someone who can provide this.

Number 9
Number 9 is the number of someone who has very strong desires for marriage. Such people will benefit a great deal from any form of partnership, whether business or personal. Care needs to be taken when choosing a spouse, though, as you tend to be attracted to people who are a good deal older than you. If your marriage partner is very much older, there is a danger that you may turn to a younger person to fulfil your needs when your spouse's physical attraction declines with age and this, of course, may cause marital disharmony.

For those who are using the Hebrew Kabala system I have included the romance numbers up to 22.

Number 10
The number 10 is the number of romance, hence you may find yourself attracted to more than one person at a time. You will probably have quite a number of love affairs before marrying and some of these are likely to be extremely passionate. Be warned, though, that sudden upsets and terminations of relationships are suffered by this number group. Most of you will eventually marry but not all such marriages are likely to prove successful and some may end in separation or divorce.

Number 11
For those with the romance number 11 the condition of marriage may be somewhat peculiar. By this I do not mean kinky or anything of that sort, quite the reverse in fact. Indeed, many of you will form strong attachments of a platonic nature and, provided this is what both partners want, these unions will be successful and satisfying. You and your partner will help each other to progress and develop in many areas of life.

Number 12
Oh dear! Those whose romance number is 12 tend to be attracted to people who are already involved with others, whether married or not. People in this group are inclined to be over idealistic about marriage, too. So you should try to find a partner who also has strong ideas of what he/she wants from a partnership yet who is more practical than yourself – and preferably not attached to anyone else, either, if at all possible!

Number 13
Unfortunately, those with the romance number of 13 tend to be attracted to people who are not very compatible with them. You may find active and energetic types interesting but, as most of you will desire to pursue

interests in a quiet and unhurried manner, this could lead to problems. After all, constant rushing about and action-packed days are great fun for a short time but pall after a while. If, however, you can find someone who is not too active and not over dominant, things will work out well for you.

Number 14
The romance number 14 is the sign of someone who doesn't enter lightly into relationships of any kind, especially marital relationships. You will be attracted by sincere people yet, even then, will proceed with caution. You are the proverbial 'once bitten twice shy' type and, once made, will expect your marriage to last for life. Should the partnership be terminated for any reason, even death, you are very unlikely to remarry.

Number 15
Number 15 is the number of those people who one always thinks of as a batchelor or spinster, not because they don't have girl/boy friends, they do yet, somehow, they simply seem unlikely to marry.

Once such people have summoned up enough courage to put their feelings into words, however, they are likely to have happy and satisfying marriages. So, if this is your number, try to choose a partner who is constant in temperament and who will stick to you in times of difficulty.

Number 16
A romance number of 16 is the sign of a flirt: someone who rushes with great speed into relationships but still enjoys flirting with others. So, you must learn to distinguish between love and obsession otherwise all sorts of problems will arise. Marriage for this group will be successful providing the subjects learn to control their flirtatious impulses early in their married lives. Once trust has built up between you and your partner, any such problem will subside considerably.

Number 17
Those with the romance number 17 should look out for a partner who is of an intellectual disposition, someone who is fun to be with but who can be serious when the situation demands it. Ideally, your partner should be domesticated but not over fussy. You may meet the love of your life while travelling or as a result of a journey, not necessarily a long one, though. People in this group may have more than one marriage in their lifetimes.

Number 18

People with the romance number 18 strongly desire comfort and therefore form relationships with those who can provide for their needs. You must take care when choosing your partner to find someone of a stable temperament who is prepared to put in as much effort as you are to make the union a success. If your romance number is 18 you and your partner will gain mutual benefit from each other in all areas of life.

Number 19

If your romance number is 19 you will be heavily influenced by your partner's financial and social status. Care will need to be taken when choosing a partner and an unwise choice may lead to considerable disappointment and unhappiness for you, your partner and your relatives. Try to choose a partner of the same social status as yourself and do not be over concerned with financial matters. Children will feature strongly in your marital life.

Number 20

The romance number of 20 usually means that you will have a short engagement and will marry soon after meeting your chosen partner. You may be attracted to rather glamorous people but know that you are unlikely to ever marry someone like this because you need a partner who has strong desires for a solid, stable home life, someone who wants a long and permanent union. Children will play an important part in the relationships of those with the romance number 20.

Number 21

Should your romance number be 21 you will wish for love and affection from your partner. However, your desire to commit yourself totally to one person may not be strong. People in this group therefore tend to have long but enjoyable engagements which may eventually end in marriage in a few cases but not in others. You must take care that your partner knows the true situation and that he/she will not be able to rush you up the aisle for some time to come.

Number 22

For those with the romance number 22 marriage will come late in life, if at all. Such a union would have to be a joint venture between both partners on all levels, including finance, business and social affairs. People with the romance number 22 will have a broad-minded outlook on love and marriage. So you are likely to have a natural desire for the companionship that a relationship brings but will not be heartbroken if a partnership did come to an end.

Year vibration

One of the ways in which numerology is used for divination is to predict what sort of year one can expect. To discover what year vibration you are on is quite simple: add up the numbers of your birthday.

For example, Alison Taylor's birth date is October 5th 1961. October is the 10th month of the year but as $1 + 0 = 1$ it should be counted as 1 in calculations, her total birth number is therefore:

$$1+5+1+9+6+1 = 23 \quad 2+3 = 5$$

Now Alison is in her 23rd year as it is 1984, so add 23 to 5 (her birth number) and you will get the year vibration: $5+23 = 28$; and $2+8 = 10$; $1+0 = 1$. Therefore Alison's year vibration is 1. This vibration number applies from her birthday on October 5th 1983 until October 5th 1984 when she will move into a year vibration of 2.

1 Vibration

If your year vibration is 1 you can expect an exciting year in which you should grow in strength careerwise. At work, a promotion or move to better things will be in the pipe-line. Now is therefore a good time to plant seeds that you will be able to harvest in later years.

This is a year in which you should branch out into new fields, so don't be afraid to grasp opportunities as they arise even if they do occur unexpectedly and catch you off balance.

During a 1 vibration year you may get married or embark on a new relationship. However, if you are happy with your present one, you will probably take up a new hobby which will become very engrossing.

2 Vibration

A number 2 vibration is a time to take stock of your situation. It is a year of learning and adjustment, a time to look closely at yourself and see if you are making use of your talents. If you discover that you have a talent which could be used more profitably, you must gather knowledge and facts about this ability during this year. So it is a very good time to enrol in an evening class, go back to college or join a society.

During the year of a 2 vibration you will find that partnerships can be made secure, this applies equally to both romantic and financial partnerships. This may be a year of marriage or, if already married, a baby.

After taking stock during a vibration year 2 you will be ready when entering year 3 to have fun. Now is the time to hot up your social life with plenty of entertainment, so accept every invitation that comes your way.

3 Vibration

If you are in a 3 vibration year you should smarten up your appearance, sharpen up your social chat and get out and be seen in all the right places. Don't worry about where the money will come from because it will come during this year. However, it might be a good idea to tuck a bit away for a rainy day.

Providing you make the most of this year to form useful contacts you will be offered new and exciting jobs.

If you wish to have a baby this is a very good vibration for such an event. Romances will blossom this year too.

4 Vibration

Phew, after all that fun last year, you will need to restore some kind of routine into your life during a 4 vibration. It is a time to get your feet firmly back on the ground. During this year you should try to tie up some of the loose ends that have been left hanging from last year.

Money may be a key factor in your life at the moment and some of you will save for a car or buy a new home while others may be saving for the forthcoming birth of children. Parenthood and financial security will be much on your mind, so it would be a good idea to have a close look at your cash-flow this year.

5 Vibration

If your year vibration is 5, you will not want to be tied down, so will change everything around you that needs changing, if you can. This may include your friends or, in some cases, even your partner. It is a time of flirtation and love affairs that are positively passionate in some cases, this may result in impulsive marriages or quick divorces.

This is the year to put all your nervous energy to a constructive use either at home or work. Sell your talents well and this will be a most productive and lucrative time. Caution must, however, be exercised otherwise something that you start for fun, such as drinking or drug-taking, may get out of hand.

6 Vibration

A 6 vibration is a time for sorting out your emotions. It is a time when you may buy a new home or start a family. This is a year of creating something beautiful in your garden, home or at work.

During this period you should try to get away to think things over and to gain peace of mind. Under this vibration travel is well favoured. At other times during the year you will need people around you with similar ideas and interests as yourself, so join or start your own groups or societies, particularly if these involve artistic or creative activities.

7 Vibration

Unfortunately the year vibration of 7 is not always an easy one to live through because, at times, you will feel like crying – go ahead, next year will be a better one!

This year may be a time of solitude but this can be put to good use if you study or develop a skill that you have been considering in the last few years. Now would be a good time to take a sabbatical as not much will be achieved at work or in business. Neither is this a good year to enter into partnerships of any kind. If you have to, however, do make sure that everything is strictly legal and above-board otherwise you could end up in big trouble.

8 Vibration

A number 8 vibration will bring an extremely active and busy year. You should achieve advancement in your career with new job offers, promotion or a job transfer coming your way. If such offers do not materialise unsolicited, no harm will come from seeking them yourself. Now is a favourable time to sign business contracts, or enter into a partnership.

During an 8 year vibration you should spend some time thinking of others who are less fortunate than yourself, so are likely to make generous donations to charitable organisations or take up community work. This year you will reap what you sow; this applies to the effort you have put into things in the past, too.

9 Vibration

The 9 vibration year is a time to finish many of the things you have started in the past before moving on to a new vibration cycle. Look back over what you have done in the last 8 years and give yourself a pat on the back for the things that have worked out well. There are many lessons to be learnt now and one of them is to let go of the past. For some people this will mean moving away from home, for others it will mean losing old friends but don't worry because you will soon make new ones.

During a 9-year cycle it is not worth starting anything new as such projects will never get off the ground properly. A 9-year cycle is one of completion, so many of your ambitions may be achieved now.

House numbers

Many people are very interested in the meaning of their house numbers – yes, houses are influenced by number vibrations too!

A house with the number 1 is most suitable for people who are single-minded and positive. This is not a suitable home for anyone who is lazy or, for that matter, indecisive. Be warned, though, that if your house

71

number is 1 you may become rather intolerant of other people, especially neighbours.

A house with the number 2 or 11 will be an ideal home for those who are co-operative but who like order in their lives. This house should help you to provide warmth and friendship to others and your home may become quite a meeting place as a result. Take care, though, that others don't take advantage of your hospitality.

Anywhere with the number 3 will be a fun home with plenty of visitors and people popping in. Children should be happy in a home with this number; in fact, it may even be a good place to start a family. However, one must learn to call a halt sometime otherwise constant to-ing and fro-ing will wear you out.

A home with the number 4 or 22 on its door will most suit people who are practical but like routine in their lives. This is a good number for a first home as it favours joint efforts. Anyone who lives at this number must take care, though, not to become too stubborn or obsessive about detail.

A number 5 house will probably be best for those who like changes – in fact, the occupants may not be there for very long before changing residence. This house number is most suitable for those who travel often or who are involved in communication. Anyone with this house number should guard against exaggeration and unreliability in order not to upset others, especially neighbours.

If 6 is the number on your front door you are likely to be a comfort-loving creature. This residence is likely to belong to someone with rather conservative attitudes but who will be a responsible and practical person. Home improvements done in or around any house with this number are likely to be very professional and tasteful.

A number 7 house is the home of a person who likes solitude, someone who likes to get away from it all. If this is your home number, you should try a little harder to get on with those around you, especially your neighbours, and not lose touch with reality.

A home with the number 8 on its door is likely to belong to those who work at home. It should provide a good atmosphere for all sorts of projects and ambitions. However, people who live at this number must take care not to work too hard, they should get out and mix with other people a bit more.

Finally, anyone who lives at number 9 is likely to be a generous, optimistic person who will make a good community leader. This may well be the home of the local scout or guide leader or a pillar of the local church. Such people must learn to keep an open mind about events that happen around them and not prejudge others though.

Do you live in the right house for you?

Place numbers

For anyone who is thinking of moving it may be of interest to find out the number of the village, town or city to which they are about to move.

To calculate the place number, again take a clean sheet of paper and write the place name on it. Under each letter write the number indicated in the chart of your chosen system. Add up the numbers. Once the place number has been worked out the meanings are the same as those for the name numbers (see pages 54 to 64).

Here are ten city names already worked out for you using the simplified Pythagorean system:

$$\begin{matrix} \text{B} & \text{R} & \text{I} & \text{G} & \text{H} & \text{T} & \text{O} & \text{N} \\ 2 & 9 & 9 & 7 & 8 & 2 & 6 & 5 \end{matrix} = 48 = 4 + 8 = 12 = 1 + 2 = 3$$

$$\begin{matrix} \text{C} & \text{A} & \text{R} & \text{D} & \text{I} & \text{F} & \text{F} \\ 3 & 1 & 9 & 4 & 9 & 6 & 6 \end{matrix} = 38 = 3 + 8 = 11 = 1 + 1 = 2$$

$$\begin{matrix} \text{E} & \text{X} & \text{E} & \text{T} & \text{E} & \text{R} \\ 5 & 6 & 5 & 2 & 5 & 9 \end{matrix} = 32 = 3 + 2 = 5$$

$$\begin{matrix} \text{G} & \text{L} & \text{A} & \text{S} & \text{G} & \text{O} & \text{W} \\ 7 & 3 & 1 & 1 & 7 & 6 & 5 \end{matrix} = 30 = 3$$

$$\begin{matrix} \text{G} & \text{L} & \text{O} & \text{U} & \text{C} & \text{E} & \text{S} & \text{T} & \text{E} & \text{R} \\ 7 & 3 & 6 & 3 & 3 & 5 & 1 & 2 & 5 & 9 \end{matrix} = 44 = 4 + 4 = 8$$

$$\begin{matrix} \text{L} & \text{A} & \text{N} & \text{C} & \text{A} & \text{S} & \text{T} & \text{E} & \text{R} \\ 3 & 1 & 5 & 3 & 1 & 1 & 2 & 5 & 9 \end{matrix} = 30 = 3$$

$$\begin{matrix} \text{L} & \text{O} & \text{N} & \text{D} & \text{O} & \text{N} \\ 3 & 6 & 5 & 4 & 6 & 5 \end{matrix} = 29 = 2 + 9 = 11 = 1 + 1 = 2$$

$$\begin{matrix} \text{M} & \text{A} & \text{N} & \text{C} & \text{H} & \text{E} & \text{S} & \text{T} & \text{E} & \text{R} \\ 4 & 1 & 5 & 3 & 8 & 5 & 1 & 2 & 5 & 9 \end{matrix} = 43 = 4 + 3 = 7$$

$$\begin{matrix} \text{N} & \text{O} & \text{T} & \text{T} & \text{I} & \text{N} & \text{G} & \text{H} & \text{A} & \text{M} \\ 5 & 6 & 2 & 2 & 9 & 5 & 7 & 8 & 1 & 4 \end{matrix} = 49 = 4 + 9 = 13 = 1 + 3 = 4$$

$$\begin{matrix} \text{N} & \text{O} & \text{R} & \text{W} & \text{I} & \text{C} & \text{H} \\ 5 & 6 & 9 & 5 & 9 & 3 & 8 \end{matrix} = 45 = 4 + 5 = 9$$

Runes

The history

Unfortunately, as I have stated elsewhere in this book, different people have different beliefs about the origin of many occult subjects and the runes are no exception. Their origin is shrouded in myth and mystery and it is one of those subjects that those in the know seem to feel needs to be protected by a great deal of secrecy.

I suppose this is hardly surprising when you learn that the word rune comes from the Norse – runar, meaning magic sign or signal; and that the ancient German word runa has two meanings, the first is secret and the second to whisper. Another word for the runes is *raunen* and the generally accepted interpretation of this old Low German word, though it has several, is to carve or cut.

But I stray, back to the origin of runes. Most people seem to hold the opinion that runes first appeared in the Bronze Age carved or cut (raunen) into rock faces. The Germanic tribes of that time, who used this type of script to communicate, travelled far and wide taking with them their rune writing. This may well be the reason that rune script can and has been found in many of the European countries including Scandinavia, Austria, Italy and Holland, to mention but a few. This well-travelled form of language even turned up when ancient burial mounds were excavated in Denmark and Sweden. In fact certain rune experts believe that the symbol for the Isle of Man may well have started life as a rune sign.

The runic alphabet, according to legend, was formulated or invented by Odin, or some call him Woden, the one-eyed god of the Scandinavian underworld. His knowledge came to him when he was suspended upside down under the world-tree, the Yggdrasil (said to be a giant ash). The Yggdrasil links the earth in one direction with the sky in the other. One of its roots travels to the land of the giants, another into the underworld and the third to the house of the gods. No wonder Odin was granted his

75

knowledge after hanging from this tree for nine days and nights without food or water, and impaled on his own sword too!

Odin, the god of occult wisdom and the protector of heroes, is pictured in many guises, sometimes as a warrior all dressed up to do battle, at other times as a bearded, old man, clad in a long, black, flowing cape and wearing a black hat with large brim to hide his face. But one thing that always remains constant about him is the description of his one good eye – a piercing, icy blue.

The rune god, as he is often called, travelled about on an eight-legged horse accompanied by two ravens and two wolves or, according to other authorities, one raven and one wolf. On his travels he used his runic knowledge and alphabet to protect and heal those he met; he also used them to keep his enemies at bay.

Different story

Other schools of thought which don't believe that the rune alphabet originated in Scandinavia hold different views about where it came from and these include the theory that runes are an adaptation of Greek letters, while others associate them with Phoenician ancestry. There are noticeable similarities between the runes and the Tarot and I Ching too, which could point to magical origins dating back to neolithic times. Whatever the case, runes are here to stay, in fact in the last few years there has been a great surge of interest in them.

Letter formation

If you study the runes closely you will at once notice that the majority of sets have no curves in the letters – they are comprised solely of straight lines. This is often attributed to the fact that they were carved or cut – not written – and it is extremely difficult to cut or carve a curve in a piece of wood or solid stone.

Making runes

Originally the runes appeared, as stated, on rock faces but the travelling tribes obviously couldn't carry these about with them, so they started to put their markings on smaller stones or rocks that were easy to carry around. As time moved on, the runes were burnt or carved out on small pieces of wood usually taken from a fruit tree. In some instances they were even engraved on to gold, bronze or copper tablets.

The most popular material today for runes seems to be wood – this should be smooth, with a good feel to it (that is very important). You should always feel at home with your runes and enjoy touching them as well as finding them pleasing in appearance. The corners of each rune are nicer to handle when rounded, but this of course is entirely a matter of personal choice. The actual letter on each rune must only appear on one side and should contain no curves or elipses. It is very easy to make your own set of runes or sets are freely obtainable from specialist shops.

If the runes are being used to cast a spell they should be written or scored on to a surface that hasn't previously been used for any other purpose, for example, a clean sheet of paper or card. However, if the spell is for the safe-keeping of an object, the runes can be reproduced on the actual object itself – for example, scratched on the inside of a ring. If the spell is requesting something from the runes they must be destroyed – and the best method is by fire – once your wish has been granted. Traditional wood, stone, metal or ceramic rune sets are not usually used for this purpose as easy destruction is not practical.

It is important to look after your runes. All runes should be kept in a specially made bag in a safe place. If you are kind to the runes they will be kind to you and give you accurate readings.

Rune poems
For those who wish to study the runes in depth there are many very good books devoted solely to this subject. In most of these are the long rune poems, rather difficult to digest or understand. None has been included in this chapter as we are only concerned here with the modern use of runes for divinatory purposes.

Reading the runes
The original meaning of casting the runes is not quite the same as today's term. In order to predict the future the runes were thrown down by the querent and any that landed with the letter uppermost were interpreted. However, if they were being used to perform a magical spell they were actually thrown at the subject.

Today, to perform a rune reading the runes are actually placed in position, although they may fall upright or reversed, however. It is of course a personal choice what formation of lay-out is used, but the most popular is a horoscope or clock formation. This is often referred to as the runic wheel. Don't feel that because the majority of people use this method, however, that you must; be brave and experiment – on your friends – until you find a lay-out that gives you good and accurate readings every time.

Beginners may find it easier if they mark the bottom of each rune so that they can see instantly when it falls in a reverse position. There is no reverse meaning for some of the runes, but more of that later.

The first runic wheel to be described here is the simplest but it will not give such a comprehensive reading as the second. First of all, find a nice large, clear surface – a table or the floor will do. Make sure that no one is going to interrupt – when learning one needs as few distractions and disturbances as possible.

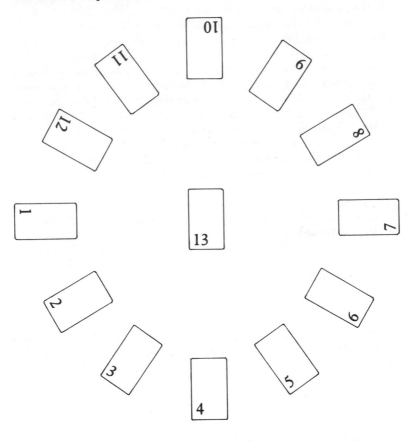

Simple runic wheel

Now clear the mind of all everyday thoughts. Place all 25 runes face down on the surface. Various schools use different numbers of runes but throughout I have started with 24 inscribed runes plus one blank one. The enquirer should then mix the runes around without turning them over (as one would when shuffling dominoes). 13 runes are chosen at random, which are then placed in a circle to look like a clock face. The first rune at 9 o'clock, the second at 8 o'clock and so on in an anti-clockwise direction until 12 runes are laid. The 13th rune is then placed in the centre of the wheel. This should always be the last rune to be put in place. If any of the runes are accidentally seen during placement the reading should be terminated and started again.

Once the runes have been placed the individual undertaking the reading should turn the runes over, starting with the first rune laid – the 1st House or 9 o'clock position. Continue around the wheel in an anti-clockwise direction and finally turn over the rune in the centre of the circle. It is not a good idea to start interpreting the runes before they can all be seen and the overall picture studied.

When reading the runes one has to study what comes before and after each rune and compare the rune in the centre with it and those opposite each other before embarking on an interpretation. If a rune is upside down, do not turn it up the correct way as reverse meanings are sometimes different from upright meanings. In this particular lay-out the runes are considered upright if their tops face the centre of the wheel. Therefore it follows that they are in reverse position if the tops are facing the outer edge of the circle.

House meanings

The *1st House* concerns the querent's personality, his/her appearance, style and attitude.

The *2nd House*. Runes falling in this position refer to the querent's possessions, ability to earn money and, in some instances, to handle money. This house also concerns financial security.

The *3rd House* will contain information about the questioner's family, his/her roots and any children he may have.

The *4th House* pertains to the home environment itself, the place of residence, house, flat or mansion.

The *5th House* concerns all to do with creativity and the subject's self-expression. This house also covers leisure time activities.

The *6th House* relates to two spheres: the first is the querent's physical health and the second refers to outside happenings and influences.

The *7th House* pertains to love and romantic partnerships. It also concerns business and financial partnerships.

The *8th House* will contain information about any deaths or inheritance which influences the subject.

The *9th House* covers education, not just in childhood but throughout life; it indicates studies to improve the enquirer's career prospects and may also contain information about travel.

The *10th House*, this house will pertain directly to the subject's career and social status.

The *11th House* should shed light on friendships and the more pleasant side of life.

The *12th House* usually indicates whether or not the querent has psychic or perceptive abilities and reveals secrets about the inner feelings of the querent.

The *13th rune* is the most important position of all because it signifies the querent.

The second runic wheel

I will now explain the second and more difficult of the runic wheel spreads before giving the meaning of each rune as these are the same for any method of lay-out used.

The second wheel uses all 25 runes. These are shuffled the same as for the first wheel but are laid out in twos in a clock-like pattern, starting at 1 o'clock then working round in a clockwise direction to 12 o'clock. The remaining rune is again laid in the centre of the circle. However, this is where it begins to become confusing for the upright position is when the top of the rune is at the outer edge of the circle and the bottom of the rune is in the centre of the clock.

The meanings of each house are the same as stated previously, but the reader must remember there are two runes per house in this lay-out.

If you don't wish to use either of these lay-outs it is perfectly acceptable for you to devise your own spread using as many or as few runes as you like. It is, however, a good idea to experiment and perfect your presentation, whatever method is used, before going ahead and giving readings to others.

The rune meanings

The modern translation is: fire or torch and it concerns protection. This glyph is associated with the zodiacal sign of Aries.

In the upright position this rune indicates new relationships. These may be partnerships of a romantic or business nature but, whichever they are, they should prove most beneficial.

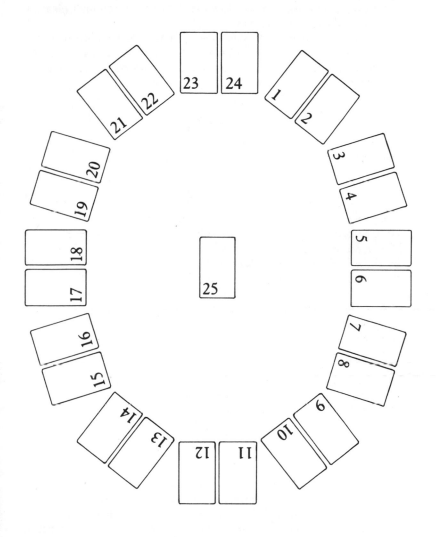

Second runic wheel

This rune is also considered to be a lucky sign for a female querent as it implies that she will be given something of value from a member of the opposite sex. For a man, it signifies that he will derive much pleasure from giving presents to a female.

The reversed meaning of this rune is a loss of friendship or the termination of a romantic attachment. It may in some instances also indicate the loss or disappearance of something considered to be of value to the querent.

The modern translation is: possessions or cattle, but as not many people now have cattle the possession interpretation is most appropriate.

This glyph is associated with the zodiacal sign of Taurus.

In the upright position this is a pleasing rune indicating romantic fulfilment. It also hints at financial gain, possibly through a legacy, tax rebate, bonus or a win on the horses.

When this rune comes up in a reverse position it indicates that the enquirer will suffer frustrations in his/her love life and that a financial gain will not live up to expectations.

The modern translation is: a journey or riding.

This glyph is associated with the zodical sign of Gemini.

When upright this is a sign of a pleasant journey, one that will bring much pleasure and joy. This journey need not be over a great distance, it may be a visit to a friend or relative or to a destination for a holiday. Whatever the case, the outcome will be a good one.

This rune when upright is also a sign of communication, so the querent may be about to receive a letter or phone call bringing good news.

When reversed this rune indicates the opposite. The querent may wait in vain for a letter or phone call. A journey or holiday may have to be postponed or cancelled at the last minute. However, should the querent actually manage to get away there will be delays en route. In this position this rune can also forewarn of visitors who turn up unexpectedly and outstay their welcome, too.

Take care when buying or selling as this is frequently a sign of an unwise deal.

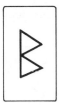

The modern translation is: a birch twig. It also translates as fertility and growth.

This glyph is associated with the zodiacal sign of Cancer.

Should this rune appear upright in a spread it indicates a pleasant event within the family – possibly an engagement or wedding celebration. As this rune is also connected with fertility it is not surprising that it shows up if a female querent is pregnant. If the querent is male, it may still indicate pregnancy if he is married and has a wife of child-bearing age.

Should the enquirer already have children, the message it gives will refer to them.

The reverse meaning of this rune indicates that the querent may be concerned over family activities or events happening within his/her social group. It also indicates difficulties regarding children or, in some instances (but tread carefully), the conception and carrying of children.

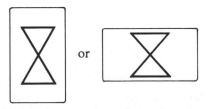

The modern translation is: prosperity and fruitfulness.

This glyph is associated with the zodiacal sign of Leo.

There is no upright or reverse for this rune. However it falls, it indicates that the querent will have a sudden and complete change in his/her life-style.

This may come as a result of his seeing the light in a certain aspect of his life. For example, this rune may indicate in a certain reading that you are going to give up your job or career to become a missionary, nun or monk. It may also signify that you are going to see the light over some puzzle that has been troubling you for some time.

This rune in some instances foretells prosperity. Care needs to be taken when interpreting this rune because its meaning will vary according to which runes lie to either side of it and what falls opposite in the lay-out.

The modern translation is: one year or a harvest.
This glyph is associated with the zodiacal sign of Virgo.

There is no upright or reverse for this rune. Whichever way up it appears, this glyph indicates that within one year of the reading the querent will reap the rewards of efforts made in the past. It is usually a sign of a job offer or promotion, but this will of course depend on which House this rune falls in.

Readers should also note that this rune frequently indicates that the subject is connected with the law in some way; for example, the querent may be a policeman/woman, lawyer or judge.

The modern translation is: a gift.
This glyph is associated with the zodiacal sign of Libra.

There is no reverse meaning for this rune, it is always a good sign whichever way up it appears. A new friendship or partnership is about to be entered into by the enquirer.

Much will be gained from this union and all those involved in it will derive much pleasure. As a result of this joint venture, a gift or gifts will be given and received by the querent.

The modern translation is: a secret or hidden thing.
This glyph is associated with the zodiacal sign of Scorpio.

In the upright position this rune refers to a secret held by the enquirer. It can also indicate that you may suddenly benefit from unexpected material gains. Such gain may come in the form of money or as information that improves your chances of obtaining your desire or achieving your goal in life.

However, when this rune appears upside down you must be prepared for a disappointment as material gains that you are expecting will not materialise and information that you receive in secret will prove totally misleading or incorrect. Do not expect too much from other people otherwise you will be disappointed.

The modern translation is: to avert or turn aside.
This is the rune of the hunting god Ullr and is said to hold avertive powers.
The glyph is associated with the zodiacal sign of Sagittarius.

There is no reverse meaning for this rune. Whichever way up it appears, it indicates that the querent will undergo a change at work which may at first seem to be a bind, but will turn out very well in the long run. This message need not just apply to work routines and may, in some cases, refer to a change of boss or working location.

On some occasions this rune will show the enquirer that a potentially difficult situation has been averted and he/she can now breathe easier.

The modern translation of this rune is: inherited possessions or property.

This glyph is associated with the zodiacal sign of Capricorn.

When appearing in an upright position it foretells of financial or material gifts for the querent, either through a legacy, will or gift from an appreciative friend or relative.

When reversed, the querent should take care while working with mechanical equipment otherwise he/she may be involved in an accident or may cause damage. Do not be alarmed by this message, though, as it does not refer to a serious event.

Readers must take care when passing this information on to the querent as everybody is different and will not necessarily react in the way expected.

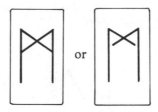

The modern translation of this rune is: man or humanity.

This glyph is associated with the zodiacal sign of Aquarius.

This rune concerns the soul, the personal welfare of the querent, humane matters and is often thought to be the rune of the New Age.

Legal documents and contracts are indicated by the appearance of this rune. It will, of course, depend where the rune falls in the lay-out as to which area of the enquirer's life these documents pertain. When in the upright position the querent should be warned that he/she will achieve the most beneficial results if signing documents after the next Full Moon.

Should it, however, be reversed it indicates that you have enemies who are just waiting on the side-lines to pounce at the next opportunity. The next rune in the lay-out will tell you how best to deal with just such people.

The modern translation of this rune is: a large deer found in Northern Europe, known as an elk, or a grass-like plant which grows in or near marshes or water.

This glyph is associated with the zodiacal sign of Pisces.

When seen in the upright position this rune signifies that the enquirer is about to take up a new interest, perhaps by accident or just for the hell of it; however, once along this road he/she will find the interest extremely stimulating. Sometimes this rune also informs the reader that the querent has a kind, giving nature and is happy to share his/her experiences with others.

Should this rune appear reversed it warns that the person having the reading must avoid people who are likely to use him/her, otherwise he will suddenly find that he is in out of his depth.

The blank rune represents the subject's karma from a previous life. It indicates the inevitable – that which is predestined and which cannot be changed.

The modern translation of this rune is: passion, it is the rune of the god Thir.

This glyph is associated with the planet Mars.

When this appears upright in a reading it signifies a passionate love affair. If the querent is male, he will fall deeply in love although he may not realise it at the time, however. If the enquirer is a female, she is a lucky lady for there is someone in her life who cares for her very much.

When this rune is in a reverse position take care, female querent, your man is the 'love them and leave them' type. If the reader puts this message across in the right way the querent will be prepared for this event when it happens.

If the enquirer is a man, this reverse rune usually signifies the dissolution of a relationship, possibly caused by a friend.

The modern translation of this rune is: fertility.

This glyph is associated with the positive aspects of the planet Venus.

There is no correct or incorrect way up for this rune. This diamond shape will appear when a subject is about to solve a problem that has been bothering him/her for some time. It also indicates a new beginning after the completion of a phase in the querent's life.

This rune frequently appears to indicate a birth or pregnancy.

The modern translation of this rune is: a horse.

This glyph is associated with the positive aspects of Mercury.

As not many people own a horse nowadays this rune can be taken to indicate transport or travel – whether a bicycle, a car or, for that matter, public transport.

A change of residence to something bigger or more suitable or a promotion or job move are on the 'cards' as it were when this rune is the correct way up.

When reversed this rune foretells of a sea journey of a beneficial nature, possibly connected with a job.

The modern translation of this rune is: fluidity.
The glyph is associated with the Moon.

This is considered by many to be the psychic rune or the rune of intuition. For most querents it indicates academic studies which have a very beneficial and lucrative result.

For female querents this rune foretells a birth.

When reversed the interpretation must be considered a warning to the enquirer that he/she must not extend himself beyond his limits otherwise he will disappoint friends, relatives and colleagues, not to mention himself. The querent may also cause damage to relationships and/or health which cannot be repaired if he pushes himself too far and ignores this warning.

The modern translation of this rune is: the Sun or life force.
This glyph is therefore associated with the Sun, naturally.

There is no reverse meaning for this rune – it simply warns that the querent must take care with health matters.

If the questioner is female and pregnant she must take rest before it becomes too late. If male or female and overworking, the message is the same – rest before you go too far.

For others who do not fall into any of the above categories, this rune warns that you must take care when undertaking physical exercise to avoid damaging your body. This rune may also warn that the querent is under nervous strain – he/she should not worry so much as all will turn out well in the end.

This is the rune of the god Odin.

The glyph is associated with the negative aspects of the planet Mercury.

This rune is associated with the older generation – it indicates that the querent will be visiting or will be visited by an elderly relative, possibly his/her parents.

When this visit takes place the enquirer will receive a gift or hear news of a gift on its way; this may be either financial or material, whichever is most likely should be indicated elsewhere in the reading.

Should this rune appear in the spread of a young person or a parent with school-age children, it indicates that there will be a scholarship to be won.

Reversed, this rune warns of an elderly relative who will prove to be rather a nuisance. An elderly person connected with the querent may become ill or begin to interfere in the business of other members of the family. This rune also indicates a wasted journey, so be warned.

The modern translation of this rune is: happiness and joy.

This glyph is associated with the negative aspects of the planet Venus.

As indicated by the modern translation, this rune is a favourable one – a sign of joy and happiness when upright.

A fair-haired man who has recently returned from travelling will enter the querent's life in some way.

If the querent is female, this man may become emotionally attached to her or her to him. If the querent is male, the acquaintanceship may concern a business relationship or just a social friendship.

Travel over water is favoured when this rune appears in a subject's spread. This travel may concern a very beneficial holiday or a business trip which brings much success.

Should this rune appear reversed, the querent must take care as a man may cause emotional problems or a female friend may let the enquirer down. If important decisions need to be taken the subject should bide his/her time for at least three days and at the most three months. Other runes in the spread should give the approximate time needed to wait.

The modern translation of this rune is: a wild ox, strength or manhood. This glyph is associated with the planet Pluto.

Opportunity is signalled by this rune. It pertains to the advancement of the querent's career; however, this won't come easily and much hard work will be needed to get results. When these results do come, though, they will bring financial rewards worth all the effort made.

When reversed, this rune indicates that the querent has missed a golden opportunity but must not dwell on this otherwise he/she will end up becoming bitter about situations that are beyond his control.

The modern translation of this rune is: Thorn, a giant or great spirit. The glyph is associated with the planet Jupiter.

A decision is pending if the rune is upright, so the querent should hold fire on his/her decision because time must pass before the situation becomes clear.

If reversed, a hasty decision will be made and regretted later; this may result in family disagreements too.

The modern translation of this rune is: necessity and constraint.
This glyph is associated with the planet Saturn.

As indicated by the modern translation, this rune warns that the querent should not act rashly. Plans will need to be carefully laid and even then there may be hold ups. Patience is the order of the day with this rune's appearance.

This rune is considered to be luckier for the old rather than the young, so it's not all bad.

When reversed, the querent is about to enter into a very risky venture. The rune next to this one should indicate what the consequences will be.

The modern translation of this rune is: natural forces which create damage.
This glyph is associated with the planet Uranus.

There is no reverse meaning for this rune. Whichever way up it is, natural forces will disrupt the querent's plans for the next year. These disruption(s) may be the death of a close friend or relative, ill health or a birth. In rare cases this rune can even indicate a forthcoming war – but that will be confirmed elsewhere in the spread. Whatever the case, there is absolutely nothing the querent can do to prevent any of these happenings.

The modern translation of this rune is: ice, which cools or impedes. This glyph is associated with the planet Neptune.

There is no reverse meaning to this rune. Whether upright or reversed, it shows a cooling or ending of emotional relationships. This is the rune of separation, of arguments both in and outside the family circle or the querent's close friends.

Scrying

The term scrying derives from the word descry, meaning to succeed in discerning – literally and figuratively – which seems a very good description of this ancient art. Most people associate scrying solely with crystal-gazing, yet it is actually a general term encompassing any form of divination which involves gazing at or into a reflective surface in order to obtain clairvoyance or, in other words, to 'see' with the mind's eye.

The practice can be traced back almost to the beginnings of civilisation and may well have begun when man first looked into a sacred stream or pool and saw reflected there clouds, shadows and light which moved to form shifting patterns that provoked oracular visions in the observer. What is certain, however, is that all the ancient cultures – the Incas, Aztecs, Mayas, Chaldeans, Egyptians, Greeks, Romans, Chinese, Hindus, Arabs, Polynesians and Australian aborigines, etc. – practised scrying in one form or another.

Scrying continues to be a very popular and easily accessible mode of divination throughout the world although it is worth remembering that, like any other divinatory art, it does require practice and dedication. So, be realistic in your expectations: don't go rushing out to buy the biggest, most expensive crystal ball you can find in the forlorn hope that you will instantly become the world's greatest seer – you won't.

Unless you have already developed your psychic abilities to the point where you are able to channel them through any medium at will, it is advisable to experiment with one or another of the simpler forms of scrying until you feel confident enough to purchase a crystal ball. Nowadays, even a small sphere made from genuine rock-crystal costs quite a lot of money so, unless you are one of the fortunate few who can 'read' the crystal first time off, it really is worth trying out one of the other methods initially.

You may, of course, find that you get such good results using whatever you have chosen as an alternative that you are quite content to continue using it; if so, fine – just carry on as you are. It matters not at all whether the medium used is a liquid, stone, mirror or crystal ball, the underlying principle remains the same in every case: the object acts as a catalyst for opening up the scryer's own psychic centres so that he/she can develop his extrasensory perception and gain insights into the past and future.

The object acting as the focal point in scrying is sometimes referred to as a speculum and many different things have been used for this purpose over the centuries. The only criteria are that such specula should possess a reflective surface – either naturally or artificially produced – and be accessible to the would-be scryer. So, what are the alternatives?

Liquids

Basically, the objects used for scrying fall into three main categories: liquids, mirrors and crystals. The first of these is, as already mentioned, probably the oldest medium used and from it has arisen several specialised forms of divination such as hydromancy and its various offshoots. As far as scrying is concerned, however, what is needed is a receptacle filled with liquid of some kind. Although expert scryers may use, and in fact have used, almost every kind of vessel and fluid imaginable, the easiest method for a beginner is to ensure that at least one of the items – container or fluid – is opaque.

For example, a very simple and effective means of scrying is to use a saucer or shallow bowl containing ink (it doesn't matter what colour this is, although beginners usually achieve the best results with black ink as they may find it easier to distinguish images against a dark background). At one time, it was quite a common practice to scry in a small pool of ink held in the palm of one's hand; and in some cultures other substances, such as molasses, oil or even blood, were used. Such practices have obvious (and messy) drawbacks and cannot be recommended!

An effective alternative, if you have a suitable container, is to pour cold, clear water into a dark-coloured, glazed pottery or glass bowl. A shallow, brass, silver or copper dish which has a smooth, polished interior makes an excellent scrying receptacle, too, as it provides a good reflective surface below the water level.

In effect, the last mentioned container could double as a scrying mirror if the concave surface is sufficiently shiny and some means can be found to suspend it. Historical evidence shows that scrying mirrors were in use long before crystal balls and enjoyed world-wide popularity as a divinatory tool. Such mirrors were not, of course, the looking-glasses with which we are so familiar today although these, too, may be used for scrying and have been since their introduction in the Middle Ages.

Mirrors

Mirror-gazing, or catoptromancy as it is sometimes called, achieved enormous publicity and some of the most famous (or infamous) historical figures of all time, such as Roger Bacon, Cornelius Agrippa, Paracelsus, Cagliostro, Nostradamus, William Lilly and – unlikely as it may seem – Catherine de Medici, included mirror-scrying among their other talents. Dr John Dee, Queen Elizabeth I's court astrologer, apparently possessed both a 'magic mirror' and a crystal ball which he referred to as his 'shew-stone' and claimed was given to him by an angel.

Scrying mirrors came in various sizes, shapes and materials but, when in use, were normally suspended or held in some way, not simply laid down on a flat surface. The ancient Chinese, for instance, used large, circular sheets of burnished bronze in which they sought answers and guidance through oracular visions. Often, the backs of such mirrors were left unpolished and the non-reflective surfaces engraved with magical or astrological symbols in order to attract the correct energies or help ward off unwanted influences. The mirrors themselves were symbolic, too, and there are reports that the Persian Magi carried mirrors as emblems of the material sphere which reflects divinity from its every part.

Many everyday ornaments, implements, weapons and utensils such as copper-bottomed saucepans or kettles were utilised as makeshift scrying mirrors if these were the only shiny, metallic surfaces available. Other items put to such usage included pieces of jewellery, highly polished stones picked up on beaches, along stream or river banks, or in fields, oiled shards of slate or even the scryer's own fingernails buffed to a pearly sheen. The list is practically endless and does credit to man's ingenuity.

Even properly prepared scrying mirrors were sometimes made from what to us now seem like unlikely materials. Dr John Dee's famous mirror, for instance, was composed of a flat, black stone of very close texture with a highly polished surface and reports vary as to whether this was a type of very fine coal, jet or obsidian.

If none of the above appeals to your imagination, a suitable alternative would be to make your own scrying mirror from an old watch or clock glass. Simply wash in luke-warm soapy water, rinse in cold water and finish off by putting a few drops of petrol, meths or other spirit on a piece of clean, soft cloth and wipe both surfaces of the glass with this to remove any last traces of grease. (Do not use detergents as these are abrasive and can scratch polished surfaces.)

When thoroughly dry, paint what will be the back of your scrying mirror, the convex surface, with a black gloss paint (model-maker's enamel is ideal and comes in tiny tins) and leave this to dry. Apply two or three coats, allowing the surface to dry thoroughly between applications, until you have obtained a really good, shiny, black surface. This will provide a cheap, effective scrying mirror and, more importantly, one that is imbued with complementary vibes because you will have made it yourself with just this objective in mind.

So, don't leave it lying around for any outsider to handle or play with, wrap it in a small piece of cloth (black silk or velvet is traditionally considered best but any new or clean material will do) and put it away safely in a box or container kept solely for this purpose whenever you are not using it. The slightly hollowed, unpainted glass backed by glossy black paint provides a good reflective surface in which to scry.

Still on the subject of mirrors, the ancient Greeks used one form of divination that combined mirror and water scrying. They lowered mirrors into sacred pools and streams: a very simple but effective exercise which can be adapted easily to modern times. All that is needed is a large transparent container of clear, cold water (a glass or pyrex mixing-bowl would be suitable) and a smooth, shiny piece of metal such as a highly polished tin lid or small hand mirror. Suspend the reflective object in the water by a piece of cotton, nylon thread or wire attached to a rod balanced across the basin top and scry into this through the water.

Crystals

Crystal-gazing, or crystallomancy to use the correct term, as we know it today has developed from a much earlier practice involving natural crystalline formations such as varieties of quartz. Initially, the natural energies contained in these crystalline structures were utilised for healing, purification rituals and protection – an application that has never died out completely and which, indeed, is enjoying something of a revival currently.

This meant that such organisms were regarded with respect and a certain degree of awe because they are recognised as embodying universal energies outside man's comprehension. So much so, in fact, that some cultures believed that the crystals themselves not only represented the forces of creation but actually contained 'spirits' in the literal rather than the figurative sense which could be communicated with and called upon to provide assistance.

It naturally followed, therefore, that crystals were treated as catalysts for 'tuning in' to these higher sources or, in modern parlance, were used for meditation, altering one's awareness or raising one's consciousness. This eventually led to them being used as foci for scrying especially as advances in lapidary techniques soon enabled even the most 'primitive' cultures to fashion them into shapes such as pyramids, spheres or ovoids which would enhance their natural properties.

Crystal balls, for example, had particular significance as they represented the crystalline 'universal or cosmic egg in whose transparent depths creation exists.' Such objects were also described as 'a proper figure of the deity previous to its immersion in matter' and signified 'the aesthetic sphere of the world in whose translucent essences is impressed and preserved the perfect image of all terrestial activity.'

These quotes may sound rather high-flown and unnecessarily flowery now yet they all convey much the same message: crystals are known to embody natural, creative forces that lie beyond the reach of man's normal consciousness but which can be contacted by altering this state – this is the basic, underlying principle of the act of scrying, but more of that later.

Natural crystals were, therefore, highly prized objects and specula made from rock-crystal (colourless quartz) or beryl (a very pale, aquamarine variety of quartz) were particularly sought after because of their Lunar associations. The Moon has always played an important role in most forms of ritual divination and this is especially so where scrying is concerned.

However, as previously stated, even a sphere of genuine rock-crystal the size of a large marble is quite costly nowadays, so what substitutes are available to the modern-day scryer? Well, some other varieties of quartz are cheaper than those already mentioned and make good scrying balls, onyx for instance. Another natural substance which can be used is obsidian – volcanic glass. And that leads on quite nicely to the somewhat misleadingly named lead-crystal which is, in fact, nothing more or less than glass with a high lead content; it does, however, make an excellent substitute.

In this plastic age, even glass is sometimes replaced by synthetic materials and it is quite usual to see so-called crystal balls made from moulded acrylics. These are very cheap and can be used for scrying but are far from ideal as their surfaces are relatively soft and easily scratched, so tend to acquire a rather dull appearance unless looked after very carefully.

Rather more suitable substitutes – but still in the inexpensive category – are those old-fashioned glass floats used by deep-sea fishermen. These hollow, glass globes can still be picked up cheaply in junk shops, especially around the coast, and are usually transparent or green. Another junk shop find worth keeping an eye out for are old, blue glass bottles which, when filled with water, make good specula.

So, as can be seen, it is possible to obtain a suitable scrying ball without plunging the holiday fund into debt! I realise that purists will be quite horrified by some of my suggestions, but it is really the purpose of scrying that is all-important and not the vehicle used.

As long as your intent is genuine and you are prepared to approach the whole subject with the right attitude, it doesn't much matter what shape your scrying implement is or what it is made from. Obviously, there are ideals in each respect but this does not mean that you cannot start scrying unless you can afford the 'proper' paraphernalia – this isn't strictly necessary, simply desirable.

Preparations

Scrying is no different from any other form of divination that has been practised for countless centuries. Over such a long period of time it has inevitably acquired numerous traditions associated with the selection, manufacture, consecration, cleansing and charging of the scrying instrument as well as rituals pertaining to its actual use.

Some of these procedures are prolonged and complicated, others brief and simple. All, however, are designed primarily to create a feeling of personal commitment – involvement, dedication and awareness – in the scryer so that he/she is in a suitably receptive frame of mind when attempting to exercise his clairvoyant/psychic faculties.

A few of the traditional recipes are now totally impractical on the grounds of cost and lack of availability, if nothing else. For example, the Abbot Trithemius (1462-1516) said: 'Procure of a lapidary a good, clear, pellucid crystal of the bigness of a small orange . . . get a small plate of fine gold to encompass the crystal round one half; let this be fitted on an ivory or ebony pedestal . . .' and so on.

Paracelsus (1493-1541) recommends: 'ten parts of pure gold, ten of silver, five of copper, two of tin, two of lead, one of iron filings, and five of mercury' and continues with injunctions on the planetary line-ups necessary before such ingredients may be put to use. I have admittedly chosen rather extreme examples yet they do serve to illustrate that it is easy to become so bogged down by ritual that the whole point of the exercise is forgotten.

Some people – ceremonial magicians for instance – will be more concerned with ritual practices that most, but this book is not intended for such practitioners and there is plenty of material available for those whose inclinations lie in this direction. I will, therefore, concentrate here on the more essential procedures and only refer to those traditional aspects that are easy to incorporate into or adapt to modern scrying methods.

This does not imply that these traditions must be adopted, simply that they may be if you, the scryer, so desire it and feel that they have significance or fit in with your requirements. So, let us suppose that you are in possession of your chosen scrying instrument and run through the preliminary steps necessary before you are ready to sit down and begin to scry.

Firstly, if you haven't already done so, make sure that the objects you intend to use are scrupulously clean. Traditionally, this is to ensure that the scrying instruments are free of any unwanted influences but, on a more mundane level, it simply means that you can be certain that you will not be hampered by trying to scry into a surface made non-reflective by a profusion of greasy fingerprints.

Remember, though, that many materials are easily scratched, so do avoid abrasive cleaning fluids, detergents and wire-wool. Crystals should be washed initially in luke-warm, soapy water, rinsed under the cold tap and, if necessary, stubborn marks removed with a few spots of surgical spirit, alcohol or similar agent before polishing with a chamois leather or soft cloth.

The idea behind keeping scrying tools boxed or wrapped in cloth away from prying eyes and probing fingers is also twofold. It delays the accumulation of dirt and grime and, on a psychic level, helps retain the vibrations/energies built up with continual usage as well as protecting your crystal ball, mirror or whatever from unwanted influences which may interfere with your next reading.

So, try not to find yourself in the situation where washing the speculum becomes a constant necessity because, if you do, it means starting from scratch and building up the required vibrations all over again each time. If prepared to take the trouble, a crystal or such like can be 'recharged' more quickly by washing in fresh, running water (not tapwater!) between the New and Full Moon. And if you can manage to find a source of water which has a high iron content, such as the Chalice Well Spring at Glastonbury, for this purpose, so much the better.

Thus armed with clean scrying implements, what else is needed? Basically, the answer to that question is very little other than a quiet place where you can perform the operation undisturbed by others and a comfortable, straight-backed chair plus a table or other solid surface on which to place your crystal, mirror or container of liquid.

Other considerations, such as lighting, incense, music, etc. are a matter of personal choice and not hard and fast rules. It is important however, to create a suitable atmosphere in which to work but how you choose to set the scene will depend on your preferences so I can only offer suggestions based on experience of others.

Method

Most scryers seem to prefer a dimly lit room, perhaps using candlelight to achieve this end. Whatever lighting is used, it is essential to avoid hard-edged shadows in the scrying medium as these can be very distracting, although some people like to angle their specula to catch the reflected light of the Moon or a strategically placed candle or table lamp.

If the room used has too bright a light or a badly positioned one, a black cloth spread over the table will help to cut down unwanted reflections or you can shield a crystal or small scrying mirror in a dark piece of material or with your cupped hands. You will probably have to experiment a bit with the positions of chair, lights, etc. until you are comfortable and can see into your speculum without strain.

Some people loathe the smell of incense or joss-sticks, others like it. If you feel that either will help create the right atmosphere, then use it by all means. Soft background music – too loud and it will distract you – can help some people to get into the right mood of relaxed concentration.

As I said earlier, it doesn't matter what props you use to create the mood, but you must be able to see into your speculum easily without sitting bolt upright in your chair and without getting a stiff neck trying to peer round corners. The idea is to sit as naturally as possible so that you feel relaxed and comfortable before you begin; and if you feel that the only way of achieving this is to sit cross-legged on the floor with your crystal ball on your lap, fine; you are the one who is going to scry, so you are the one who needs to feel comfortable.

Once everything is positioned to your satisfaction, sit quietly for a few minutes and allow yourself to unwind. If you already practise meditation, five to ten minutes of this would prepare you mentally and psychically for what you are about to attempt. Novices should just spend the time in quiet contemplation; try not to start worrying about whether or not you left the car lights on, posted the football pools coupon, or what to buy for dinner tomorrow, just relax and consider what you hope to achieve with your scrying sessions.

The object of this transition period is to prepare you mentally, physically, emotionally and psychically so that you are at your most receptive: relaxed and tranquil but open to any impressions that may manifest and in the right frame of mind to accept these if they occur but not feel disappointed if they don't. Your attitude, your receptivity, is important.

Try not to expect too much. Even experienced scryers have 'off days' when their intuitive powers seem to have deserted them, when they receive no impressions, nothing seems to come through, no images appear and the scrying sessions have to be aborted, put off to another day. No one can be 'sensitive' all the time and, indeed, it is unlikely that anyone would want to be either. So, ideally, one needs to be able to control one's sensitivity, to channel it, to learn how to tune-in when it is desirable and not when it is inconvenient.

This is exactly what scrying is all about: it is a method of developing one's clairvoyant faculties, one's innate intuition or sensitivity – call it what you will. Everyone has such abilities, to a greater or lesser degree, but not everyone is aware of this fact and even fewer bother to develop them. Scrying is one way of doing so; there are others, of course, and you may find that another method suits you better. But scrying is relatively cheap and easy to carry out in your own home, so it is worth giving it a try at least.

As I said earlier, don't be put off if nothing seems to happen the first time you do try. Like any other method of psychic development, it takes time to achieve results. With practice, however, you should find that it becomes increasingly easy to get into the right mood for scrying. Even after one or two attempts, you will probably reach the stage where you can achieve and maintain that 'half-way' state between waking and sleeping quickly and naturally without undue effort.

This is the crux of the matter. The whole process should be a natural one; there is no need to force the issue, let it flow smoothly and naturally until you feel ready to begin. Then, and only then, look into your scrying medium. Again, don't try too hard, just let your eyes focus on the centre of the crystal (or whatever is being used) for a moment, then allow your gaze to relax slightly so that you can still see the crystal but are not consciously aware of its boundaries.

It's a terrible temptation for beginners to stare fixedly at their crystal balls, willing something to happen so hard that tears form in their eyes as they try desperately not to blink, their jaws clamp together and their bodies become rigid with the effort of it all. I know – it happened to me the first couple of times! So, if you feel yourself becoming tense, remove your gaze, sit back and relax for five minutes before trying again. If, however, your second attempt proves unsuccessful, try again another day.

This sort of exercise can be very tiring if you are unused to it, so it is silly to keep on to the point of exhaustion and be so disillusioned that you give up the idea completely. It's much better to extend the length of your scrying sessions gradually because you are much more likely to meet with success if you are feeling alert and confident rather than tired and depressed.

Expectations

Now, what can you expect to see? Well, you may not see anything at all except a rather blurry image of a crystal ball of course. On the other hand, some people are lucky enough to be able to scry successfully at their first attempt. Everyone is different, each of us is an individual, so what we are likely to experience when we scry will vary from person to person.

The most common indication of a potentially successful scrying session, though, is that the crystal (or whatever is being used) will appear to cloud over, become misty or foggy. The fogging may increase steadily, becoming denser and darker until the scrying medium appears to be black; or there may be a great deal of movement, a swirling mist of wispy tendrils that gradually evolve into a milky opacity.

This is the point where things really begin to happen so, if you get this far on your first attempt, there is good cause to feel hopeful that you possess good clairvoyance. Some people have to have several scrying sessions before reaching this stage, though, so don't be too discouraged if there is no appreciable change in the speculum's appearance. Or, of course, it may be that you will not 'see' in the crystal at all, no matter how many times you try, and even this fact need not indicate that you cannot scry.

As I said before – and must emphasise – there are no hard and fast rules to successful scrying and each individual will experience it in a different way; all I can do is describe some of the possibilities based on my and other people's experiences.

So, assuming for a moment that your scrying medium has reached the 'dense' stage, what may happen next? Some people become aware of vague, shadowy shapes or figures which gradually grow sharper and brighter, more clearly defined until, eventually, it is possible to distinguish every detail. This process is similar in effect to looking at something through a camera and, without removing your eye from the viewfinder, making adjustments until the whole scene comes into sharp focus.

One variation of this process is for small points of light to break through the crystal's density. These get larger and brighter until the whole thing seems to be glowing with light, perhaps accompanied by flashes or bands of colour. Some people even describe the speculum as pulsating with light and colour before the images appear, often quite quickly. Or the brightness may spread out from the centre of the crystal and be surrounded by a ring of colour, rather like a circular rainbow. This latter phenomenon is explained by some authorities as seeing the crystal's aura, which seems apt.

So far, I have only described what may happen for those who actually see images in the speculum itself, but what of those who don't? Should they, perhaps, give up every attempt to scry? Not yet! It takes some people longer than others to achieve a breakthrough, especially if they have not tried to exercise their latent psychic abilities before. Unless you are a 'natural' – and not many are – it does take time to learn how to 'open up' your sensitivity. Like anything else worth while, most people have to work at it so, the more often you practise, the easier it will become.

It is also possible that your clairvoyance takes a slightly different form and, instead of seeing images in the speculum, you will see them in your mind's eye. If so, the crystal ball will remain a crystal ball but the act of gazing at it will trigger off mental images just as vivid as those that can be seen in a crystal. The fact is, clairvoyance may be experienced subjectively as well as objectively, therefore some scryers see mental images while others see actual pictures or scenes in the chosen scrying medium.

Both are equally valid; indeed, they are but different manifestations of the same phenomenon. But what of the images themselves? Even here, messages can be conveyed in a variety of ways. Some cases of subjective scrying, for example, can be likened to those convincingly realistic dreams where, upon waking, the dreamer finds it hard to believe that he has been asleep and not actually experiencing the events in his dream.

The method of interpreting such mental imagery is, again like dreams, to take especial note of the impression created and to regard this as the prime message of the scrying experience. In other words, was the overall impression one of happiness, worry, expectancy or what? It is important to consider this aspect first because the actual sequence of events depicted must be assessed against this background and may be translated as being symbolic rather than literal visions of what has passed, is happening now or is yet to come.

Objective clairvoyance may also be symbolic, the scryer may see symbols rather than scenes in the crystal. Others liken their scrying experience to watching a trailer to a film – a series of apparently disconnected scenes. Here the difficulty is to find the story-line, to make the connection between one scene and another. Sometimes, too, the projectionist seems to have got the reels mixed up because it turns out that one or two of the shots are clips from another film but, because the same person or location appears in several of them, you are fooled into supposing you are seeing the trailer to only one film when in fact this is not so.

Oddly enough, this problem may have a rational explanation. Usually what is happening is that you are seeing events out of sequence, perhaps the first scene depicts something from the past, the next is in the future, the third, fourth and fifth revert to the past, the sixth is the present and so on. A few questions put to the person for whom one is scrying will normally enable you to sort out the timing of events shown in this way.

In any case, once you have some experience of scrying, you will probably find that it becomes easier to recognise what is relevant and what is not. At first, it is quite usual to receive impressions where not all the objects seen belong to the same time frame or, indeed, pertain to the querent; other influences may impinge on the client's reading and the images seen – or at least part of them – may not 'belong' to that person's life at all.

Again, don't worry because it does get easier to recognise this sort of 'psychic interference' and you will quickly learn to ignore such irrelevances with practice. You may not, of course, be bothered by this problem at all. Your scrying may be sequential, one vivid scene fading into another which becomes brighter and clearer until every small detail can be seen. If so, consider yourself fortunate because you will then be able to relate the reading directly to the client. Or you may, perhaps, perceive objective images in the crystal and receive subjective impressions in your mind simultaneously so that you can interpret what is seen rationally, even if the visions are symbolic.

It really doesn't in the least matter how you receive your impressions or what form the pictures take. The important thing is whether or not you are able to interpret them accurately: the scrying must have a meaningful outcome in order to be regarded as successful.

Summary

Ensuring that you are in the most receptive mood possible before commencing to scry will help, so will a knowledge of symbolism (especially dream symbolism). The trappings do not matter, these are all a question of personal preference and only experience will indicate what works best for you. So do experiment, try out some of the suggestions in this chapter or think up some ideas of your own.

At first, it is usually better to try scrying on your own but, once you begin to get results, ask a friend to help because confidence will build more rapidly once you start scrying for someone else; besides, you are going to have to learn how best to convey information to others without causing them anxiety or fear. You may find it easier to read for someone else if you ask the other person to place his/her hands round the crystal or whatever for a few moments so that it absorbs his vibrations, forging a link between client, scrying medium and seer. You may not need or wish to do this, only experience will tell.

Your attitude towards scrying is, however, the single most important fact of all. If you don't expect anything to happen, it won't. Why should it if you are putting up barriers, closing your mind even to possibilities? On the other hand, if you expect something to happen it will be because you will be receptive, open to impressions outside the self, able to break through to those realms which are beyond man's normal comprehension.

Don't be frightened by this prospect, there is nothing abnormal about it, quite the reverse, it is the most natural thing in the world. We are all part of nature which, in turn, is but a small part of the greater whole and scrying, like any other form of divination, is simply one method of tapping into this vast source of knowledge – naturally.

Glossary

Acuto-manzia

divination using 13 tacking pins (10 straight and three bent). Most frequently used to predict the future.

Aeromancy

not an easy form of divination because one has to consider atmospheric conditions including cloud shapes, spectral formations, comets and, according to some authorities, UFOs. This is no longer a fashionable form of divination however.

Ailuromancy

those that are fond of cats will enjoy this method of divination because one has to study the actions of a cat or cats.

Alectryomancy

a black hen, white game-cock or sacred chicken pecks corn from a circle of letters; an alternative is to recite the alphabet until the cock crows on a letter which is then used as the basis for a prophecy.

Aleuromancy

or the reading of fortune cookies, as they are now known. Possible answers to questions are written on small pieces of paper then baked in a ball of dough.

Alomancy

this kind of divination may have given rise to present-day superstitions about spilling salt. Alomancy is the art of predicting events in patterns made by salt that has been sprinkled.

Alphitomancy

a conscience tester: anyone with a clear conscience is able to eat the special cakes used in this obscure form of divination but those with guilty consciences find the cakes unpalatable.

109

Anthroponmancy	is a form of human sacrifice, happily no longer practised.
Apantomancy	forecasts are made by the chance meeting of animals or birds. A good example is a black cat crossing one's path.
Arachnomancy	not everyone's favourite subject – spiders. Divination from the appearance and behaviour of spiders.
Arithmancy/ Arithmomancy	these are really other names for numerology.
Astragalomancy	divination by casting bones, usually the vertebrae or ankle bones of sheep.
Astraglomancy/ Astragyromancy	the interpretation of tiles bearing letters or, in some cases, numbers which has developed into dice reading.
Astrology	can be used as a method of divination.
Augury	this is the general art of divination, using all forms of prophecy.
Austromancy	this method of prediction is carried out by studying the wind. An example is the saying, 'the North wind shall blow and we shall have snow'.
Axinomancy	take care when using this kind of divination as axinomancy means the use of a hatchet or axe to answer questions.
Belomancy	this is considered to be one of the oldest forms of divination and involves the firing or balancing of arrows.
Bibliomancy	judging by the name of this art one would assume that the Bible was probably the first book used. Bibliomancy is the art of divination by using a book (nowadays any book can be picked at random), opening it up and the first words you read give the answer to your question. It works too!

Bone throwing	what more explanation does this require? It is also known as astragalomancy.
Botanomancy	leaves and branches are used to perform this form of divination.
Capnomancy	this may have been practised by Indians because it is the study of smoke rising from a fire.
Cartomancy	this is fortune-telling using cards, either Tarot or playing cards (*see* pages 9-37).
Cartopedy	a ticklish business this – predicting the future and assessing the character from the soles of the feet. Said to be used by emperors to choose a bride.
Catoptromancy/ Catoxtromancy	and early form of crystal-gazing. A mirror was turned to the Moon to catch the Lunar rays or suspended in water and the reflections read.
Causimomancy	back to the fire again. Causimomancy is a romantic form of divination. All you need is a nice roaring fire to cast a few objects into – if they fail to ignite or if they burn really slowly then it is a good omen. If they flare up quickly, at least they will keep you warm while they last!
Cephalomancy	divination using the skull or head of a donkey or goat.
Ceraunoscopy	this is the study of thunder and lightning.
Ceromancy/ Ceroscopy	is the art of bubble-reading; that is the shapes that form when you pour melted wax into cold water.
Chaomancy	divination from aerial visions.
Cleidomancy/ Clidomancy	a form of dowsing. A key is suspended on string or cotton and provides a yes or no answer to questions put to it.
Cleromancy	this is similar to divination with dice, but you use pebbles or wooden counters drawn from a pot or cast on the ground. Beans can also be used.

Coscinomancy	this is similar to cleidomancy except that a sieve is used – a housewife's version, I suppose.
Crithomancy	corn, grain or barley cakes are studied for an omen.
Cromniomancy	the question posed and possible answers are written on paper and attached to onions which are then placed on an altar. The first onion to sprout provides the correct solution to the problem. Onion skins can also make wishes come true, apparently, just toss them in the fire and make your wish.
Crystalomancy	a term for crystal-gazing.
Cyclomancy	divination from a turning wheel.
Dactylomancy	this kind of divination was often used to find the sex of an unborn child. A ring (most often the pregnant lady's own wedding ring) is dangled over the stomach and, depending on how it swings, the sex of the child is prophesised.
Daphnomancy	laurel branches are placed on an open fire; the louder they crackle the better the omen.
Demonomancy	divination using demons.
Dendromancy	omens associated with oak and mistletoe.
Dice	often used for divination.
Dominoes	closely related to dice. It is easy to learn divination with dice and dominoes.
Entomomancy	bit creepy this one: making predictions from the appearance and behaviour patterns of insects.
Face reading	this is known as physiognomy.
Felidomancy	divination from the behaviour or actions of a cat. (See ailuromancy).
Floromancy	the study of flowers.
Foot reading	see cartopedy.
Gelomancy/ Geloscopy	don't laugh – this is divination from the tone of someone's laughter.

Genethlialogy	the future can be predicted by the influence of the stars at the time of birth.
Geomancy	its original meaning is divination from the pattern made by sand, dust or dry soil thrown down. But some say geomancy has moved on and includes readings from dots made randomly on paper with a pencil or even doodles.
Gyromancy	something for those who have had one too many. The prophecy is spelt out when someone walks in a circle marked with letters until they become dizzy and stumble at different letters.
Halomancy	another term for alomancy. The only difference is that the salt is cast into a fire.
Haruspicy/ Hieromancy/ Hieroscopy	these are all concerned with drawing prophetic conclusions from objects of ancient sacrifice.
Hippomancy	if you are able to make prophecies from the actions of horses, you are performing hippomancy.
Hydromancy	tea-leaf and coffee ground readings developed from hydromancy which is the art of divination using water. The ebb and flow of the water, the colour, the ripples produced when you drop a stone into it are all part of this art.
I Ching	a very ancient form of Chinese divination based on hexagrams that are formed line by line through a procedure involving yarrow stalks or coins. Once the hexagrams are formed, the querent refers to the *I Ching* or *Book of Changes* and refers to the text for guidance.
Ichthyomancy	apparently the shape of fish can be used for divination.
Itches	on the body can have different meanings depending where they are. For example, an itch on the left palm indicates money coming in and on the right palm money going out.

Knives/scissors	much information can be gained from these items. How they land when you drop them will indicate good or bad omens, so too will the way you hand them to others.
Lampadomancy	apparently an oil lamp or torchlight can be used as an indicator of good or bad omens.
Lecanomancy	another form of hydromancy, only in this case stones or gems are dropped into the water.
Libanomancy/ Livanomancy	is interpreting omens from the smoke that rises from incense.
Lithomancy/ Lethomancy	divination using precious gems of different colours. For example, red stones denote romantic happiness, black indicate misfortune and blue prophesy good luck. Coloured glass beads can be used if gems are not available.
Lychnomancy	this is where the candelabra comes into its own. Lychnomancy is divination using the flames of three candles.
Margaritomancy	I can't really see why this form of divination was ever used. A pearl was dropped and, if it bounced, it was supposed to mean that a guilty person was approaching.
Metagnomy	this is a comparatively modern type of divination. A subject is hypnotised and future events, things that have happened in the past and general scenes provide the information for the reading.
Meteoromancy	divination from shooting stars and meteors.
Metopomancy/ Metoposcopy	character readings from the lines on a person's forehead.
Mirror gazing	see catoptromancy.
Moleoscopy	the art of reading moles on the body. This was a popular type of reading in the 16th and 17th centuries.
Molybdomancy	molten lead or tin should be dripped into cold water and the shapes produced form the basis for the reading.

Myomancy	mice or rats are studied. Their movements, colouring, etc., are all considered carefully then predictions made.
Necromancy	this is not very nice – it means predicting through communicating with the dead.
Nephelomancy	divining the future from cloud formations.
Numerology	a method of interpreting dates and names in terms of numbers and forecasting events past and future from them.
Oculomancy	they say you can tell much from people's eyes. And that's what oculomancy is all about.
Oenomancy/ Oinomancy	another form of divination involving liquid. In this instance the predictions are made from wine that has been poured and offered to the gods.
Oneiromancy/ Oniromancy	a posh way of saying dream interpretations.
Onomancy/ Onomatomancy	the meaning of someone's name or the letters in that name. Not really divination.
Onychomancy/ Onyomancy	this has connexions with palmistry because it is the study of finger-nails in sunlight. And onyomancy is the interpretation of a subject's character from finger-nails.
Oomantia/Ooscopy/ Ovomancy	divination using eggs.
Ophiomancy	snakes or even serpents can be used to forecast what will happen in the future.
Orniscopy/ Ornithomancy	both concern the omens given by the flight of birds.
Pegomancy	spring water or the bubbles produced by a fountain are what are read for pegomancy.
Pessomancy/ Psephomancy	while you are looking in the spring at the water take a look at the pebbles there too, because readings can be made through the study of such pebbles.
Phyllorhodomancy	a form of divination dating from ancient Greece. Rose petals were slapped against the

hand and the amount of noise produced when so doing determined how successful a specific venture would be.

Psychometry	this type of divination is becoming increasingly popular. It is the art of predicting events, etc. from an object, often a piece of jewellery.
Puto-mani	an ancient method of divination concerning the shoulder-blade of a deer.
Pyromancy/ Pyroscopy	these are both forms of divination using fire.
Rhabdomancy	this is the art of divination by means of a stick; some authorities believe a wand was also used. It possibly refers to an early form of divining rod.
Rhapsodomancy	similar to bibliomancy except that a poetry book is used and a whole poem may be referred to and not just a word or two.
Runes	an early form of alphabet also used for divinatory purposes (*see* the chapter on runes, pages 75-93).
Sand reading	the same as geomancy.
Scapulomancy/ Spealomancy	not very pleasant this: predictions made from the cracks that appear in the burnt shoulder-blades of animals. Sometimes the shell of a tortoise was used.
Sciomancy	this is a term used for divination with the assistance of spirits.
Scrying	crystal-gazing (*see* pages 95-107).
Selenomancy	interpreting the appearance and various phases of the Moon.
Shadow reading	this was practised extensively in the Far East. Palms and shadows are measured and studied.
Shell reading	not many people practise this art but there are a few left who can do readings from sea shells. They are also used by others as amulets – not always consciously though.

Sideromancy	apparently one can predict the future by burning straws on a hot iron and studying the shapes thus produced.
Solistry	this is the ancient art of foot reading.
Sortilege	comes from the Latin *sors*, meaning lots. Sortilege is divination by the casting of lots in the hope of a good omen. Tossing a coin is one form of sortilege.
Spodomancy	cinders or soot may also give an indication of what's to come.
Stareomancy	divination from the traditional elements: earth, water, air and fire.
Stichomancy	another form of bibliomancy.
Stolisomancy	apparently it is possible to draw omens from oddities in the way people dress. (Just how I'm not quite sure).
Sychomancy	a message is written on a leaf taken from a tree and the slower it dries the more favourable the outcome.
Tasseography	this is a very ancient art which probably originated in China. The Romans were said to read the residue left in a goblet after drinking wine. You can also use coffee grounds to undertake a reading. Drink nearly all the drink then swirl the remainder around the cup (clockwise three times), turn the cup upside down on a saucer or plate, then study carefully the shapes formed by the grouts.
Tea-leaf reading	also known as tasseography.
Tephramancy	tree bark is burnt and the diviner reads the ashes in a similar way to tea-leaves.
Tiromancy/ Tyromancy	divination using cheese.
Xylomancy	there are two methods of divination which come under xylomancy, the first concerns the burning of wood. Omens are formed by the speed at

which the wood burns. The second is to do with the picking up of wood – the interpretation of its shape and formation.

Zoomancy   as the name suggests, this concerns the study of animals. Their behaviour and appearance are considered in order to prophesy what will happen in the future.

Index

prediction

THE MAGAZINE FOR ASTROLOGY AND THE OCCULT

... is a popular style magazine for those interested in astrology and all aspects of the occult. It is published on the second Friday of each month and contains regular features on the Tarot, graphology, palmistry, dream interpretations, book reviews and a 16-page astrology section including Sun sign forecasts for the month ahead as well as feature articles on a wide range of occult and related subjects.

68 pages or more monthly, illustrated and carrying advertisements—including a directory of psychics and consultants, groups, societies etc—PREDICTION represents incredible value for money and offers readers several services including two free ones: Occult Question Time and Personal Classifieds, so why not buy a copy now?

Available from all leading newsagents. In case of difficulty, write to Prediction Magazine, Link House, Dingwall Ave, Croydon CR9 2TA. Telephone 01-686 2599  A Link House Publication